CW01113128

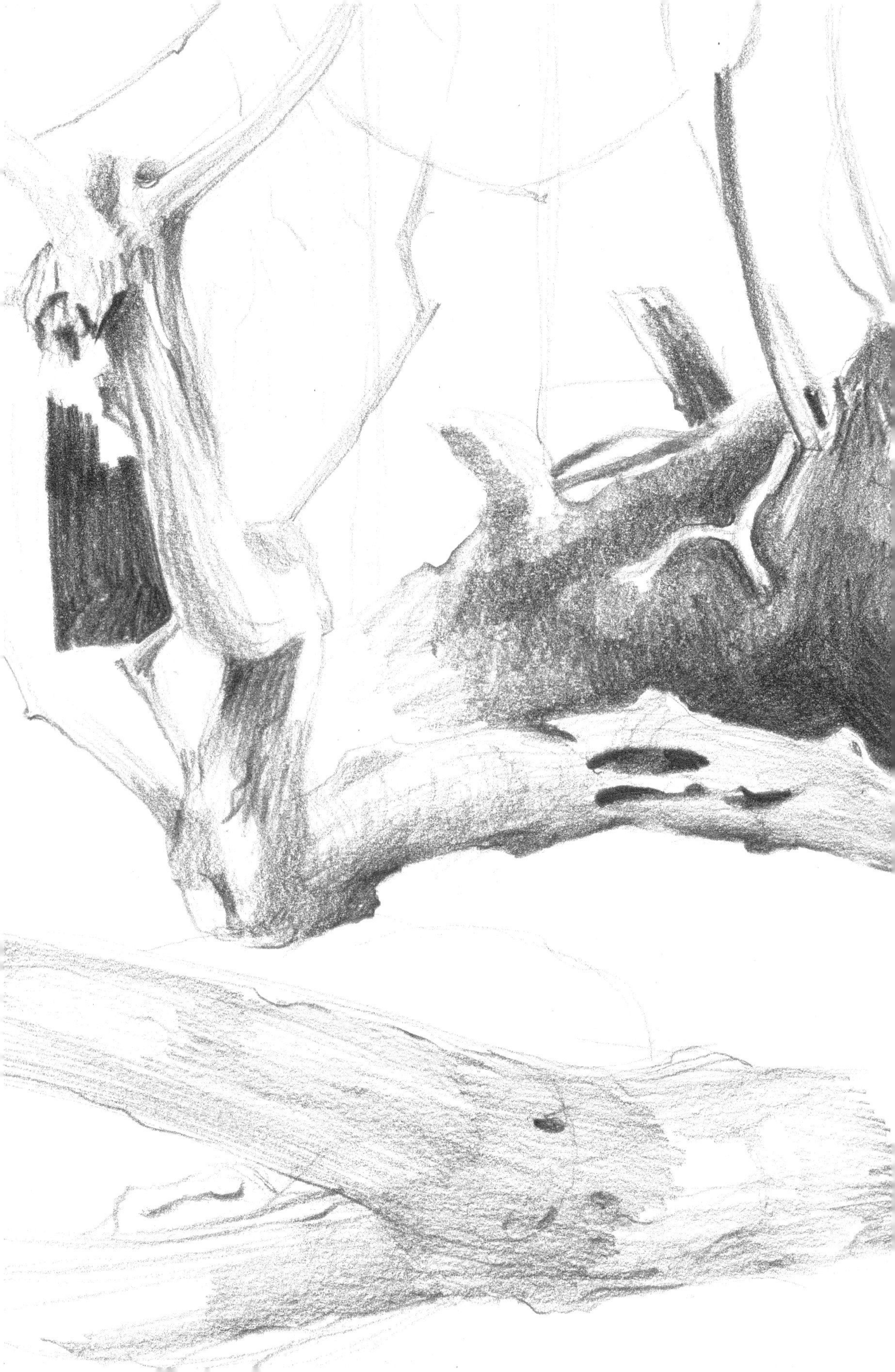

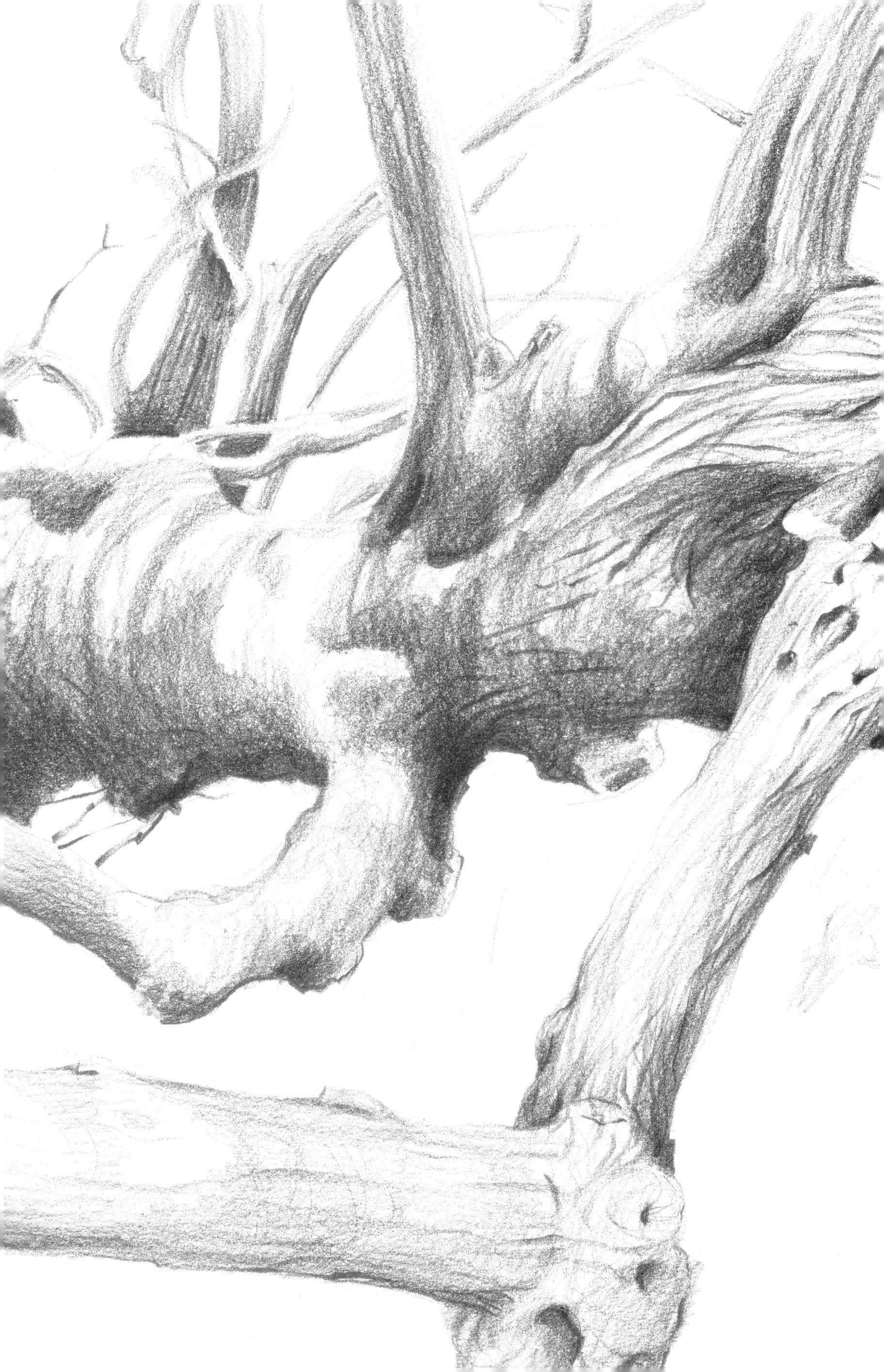

Evergreen and Eighty

Poems by Bob Breach

Drawings by Chris Gregory

To my best ever student, of long ago

Bob Breach.

2008
The Melbury Press

First published in 2008

The Melbury Press,
Ivy Paddock,
Melbury Abbas,
Shaftesbury,
Dorset.
SP7 0DW

Copyright © Bob Breach 2008
Drawings copyright © Chris Gregory 2008

All rights reserved. No part of this publication may be reproduced, stored in a retrieval system, or transmitted, in any form, or by any means, without the prior permission of the author, c/o The Melbury Press.

ISBN 0 9533347 1 6

Typeset in Ariel
Typesetting and design by John Breach & Mark Barrett

Printed by Salisbury Printing, Greencroft Street, Salisbury SP1 1JF

*All profits from the sale of this book
will be given to the charity
Support for the Oppressed Peoples of Burma
(SOPB).*

Burma:
In memoriam Padoh Mhan Sha, assassinated 2008

DEATH OF A QUIET MAN

All those violent ends
Documented in my living years
Gandhi, Kennedy, Luther King,
Indira and her son, Aung San,
Benazir and her father
All standing up to lead.

Now a quiet Karen, exiled
From his home in Burma,
Padoh Mhan Sha, a man of peace
Stood up to lead
A solitary calling, his wife dead,
His children far away.

Sharing food with him, and hope
That precious spark, and talk,
Makes this violent end
So different from all the others.
Shot to death alone
Sitting in the sun on his verandah.

Weep and remember Padoh Mahn Sha,
Weep and remember Burma.
And then stand up to lead
Against the assassins,
Against the dictators,
For peace, for peace, for peace.

Juliet Rogers

CONTENTS

Spring

Enter Spring Suddenly	3
In Memoriam Bill Purbrick	5
A Frosted Magnolia	7
A Walk on Breeze Hill	9
When Samantha Died	11
Wincombe Lane Re-cycling	13
Mozart and Marriage	15
The Future of Daffodils	17
Ash Wednesday: Compline	19
I Shall Walk in my Garden	21
Hospital Odstock	22
May Morning	25

Summer

June Walk	29
Concert Port Regis	31
Tennyson Down	33
New House in the Lane	35
At an Exhibition: Iris Stylosa	37
Westminster Hospital Shaftesbury	39
A Rose Song	41
Committee	43
Golden Wedding	45

Autumn

End of Summer	49
A Hundred Crows	51
In the Lane	53
An Autumn Walk	55
In Memoriam	57
Late November	59
Black Dog	61
In Praise of Tennis	63
Encounter	65
A Bird in the Road	67

Winter

Colours in a Melbury Landscape	71
After the Great Storm	73
December Day	75
Rugby on TV: Ireland v. England	76
The Day They Took the Calves Away	79
Silences	80
Spring Delays	83
Four Sunsets and a Sunrise	84
Sue, on her Eightieth Birthday	87

SPRING

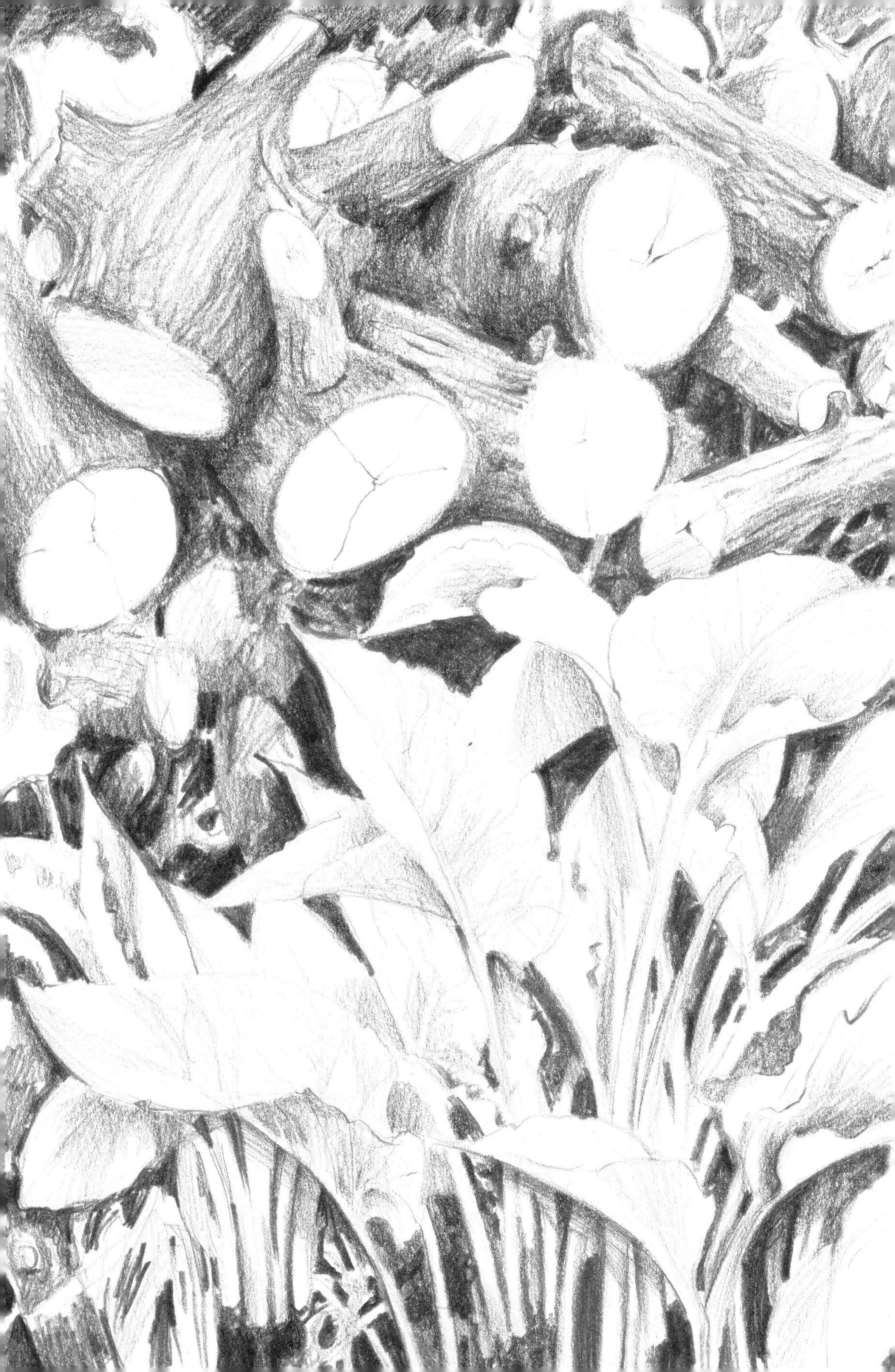

Enter Spring Suddenly

Spring turns up one day, shunting out winter
No hints, no nods or intimations
That brown and soup-like skyline splinters
Shattered, lost in unknown destinations
Though winter hangs on still in gardens, unwinding
Iris stylosa, the early heathers
Hellebores turned tatty, now declining
Sticky chestnut buds from colder weather

Poets cliché love and dancing daffodils
The primrose, violets and celandine
Hyacinths in pots adorn the kitchen cills
While housewives hang the winter's sheets on line
Birds are singing loud for partners
Flashing from black-burdened boughs of ash, talk,
How swift, how purposeful are those darters
Defy the watching, static sparrow hawks.
The lusty buzzards sail in pairs as small as high
Across and through the arriving skies
Seeking exactly the exactly site
To breed a brood before the impulse dies.

This warming sun, does this explain it all ?
So casual and spattered with cold rain
This mystery why seasons rise and fall
Why earth should stir and snowdrops line the lane.

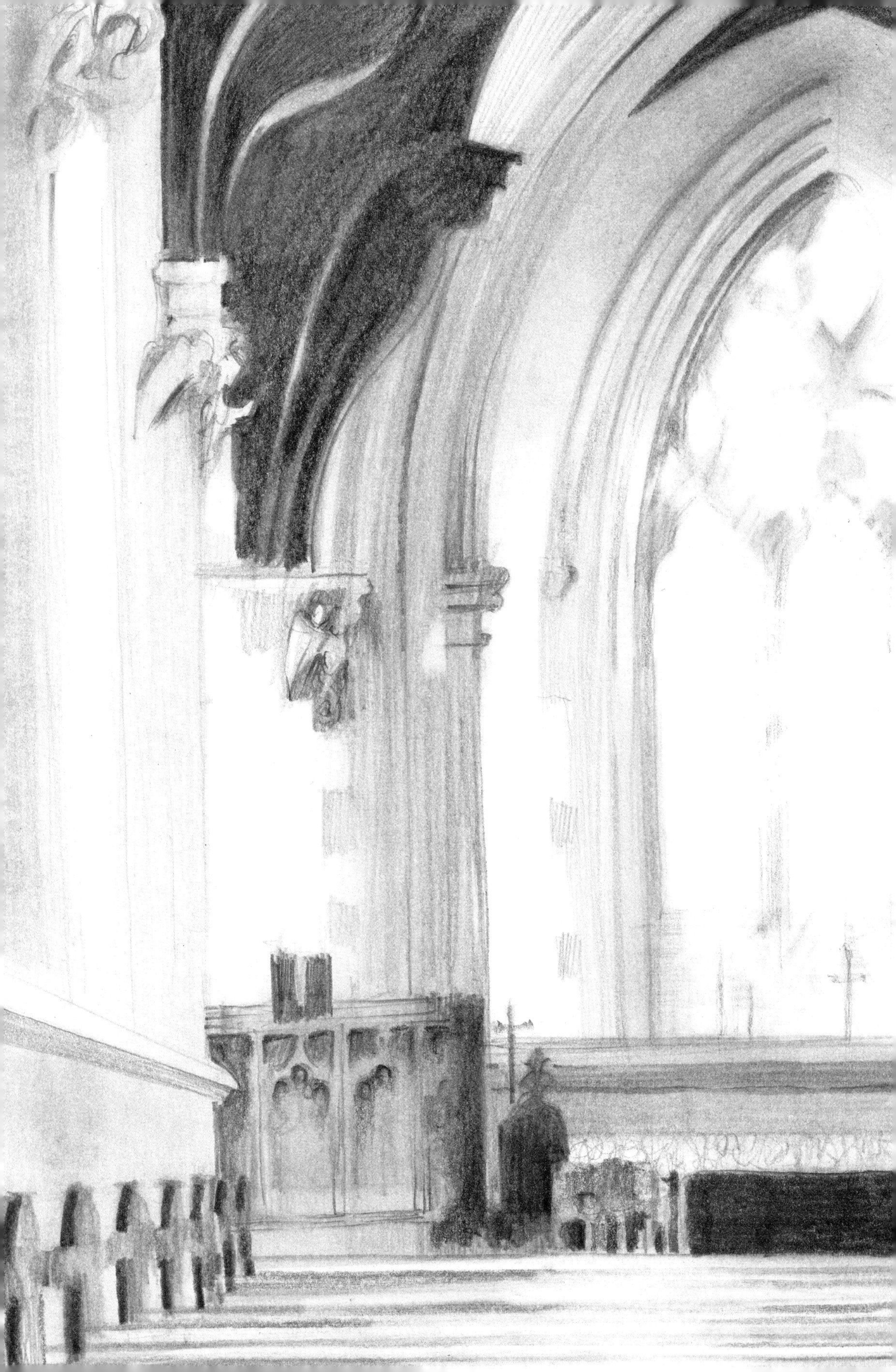

In Memoriam: Bill Purbrick

He died at the chilly pivot of the year
Spring's growings breaking through the brown
Frame of winter, the lawn not mown.
All the usual things that he held dear around him
Dancing daffodils, the piercing pinnacles of hyacinths
Heathers purple as the altar frontals
The rusty leaves of a rose taking the air.
The chances they take!
The blackthorn winter and the sudden frosts.

Bill, he was a thruster through the browns of life,
A noisy, funny, rumbustious man's man
Defying negatives, striking them with strong arms
Bending circumstance to his insistent will
Till his blackthorn and that sudden frost.

He resisted the universe
Turned diagnosis on its fallible head
Holding his place high.
But, die he did, not wishing so
Holding a life reduced a true life still.

Accidents happen the world says
Blackthorns and cold winds.

Today the spring sun is warm
Bill's God receives him.

April 2006

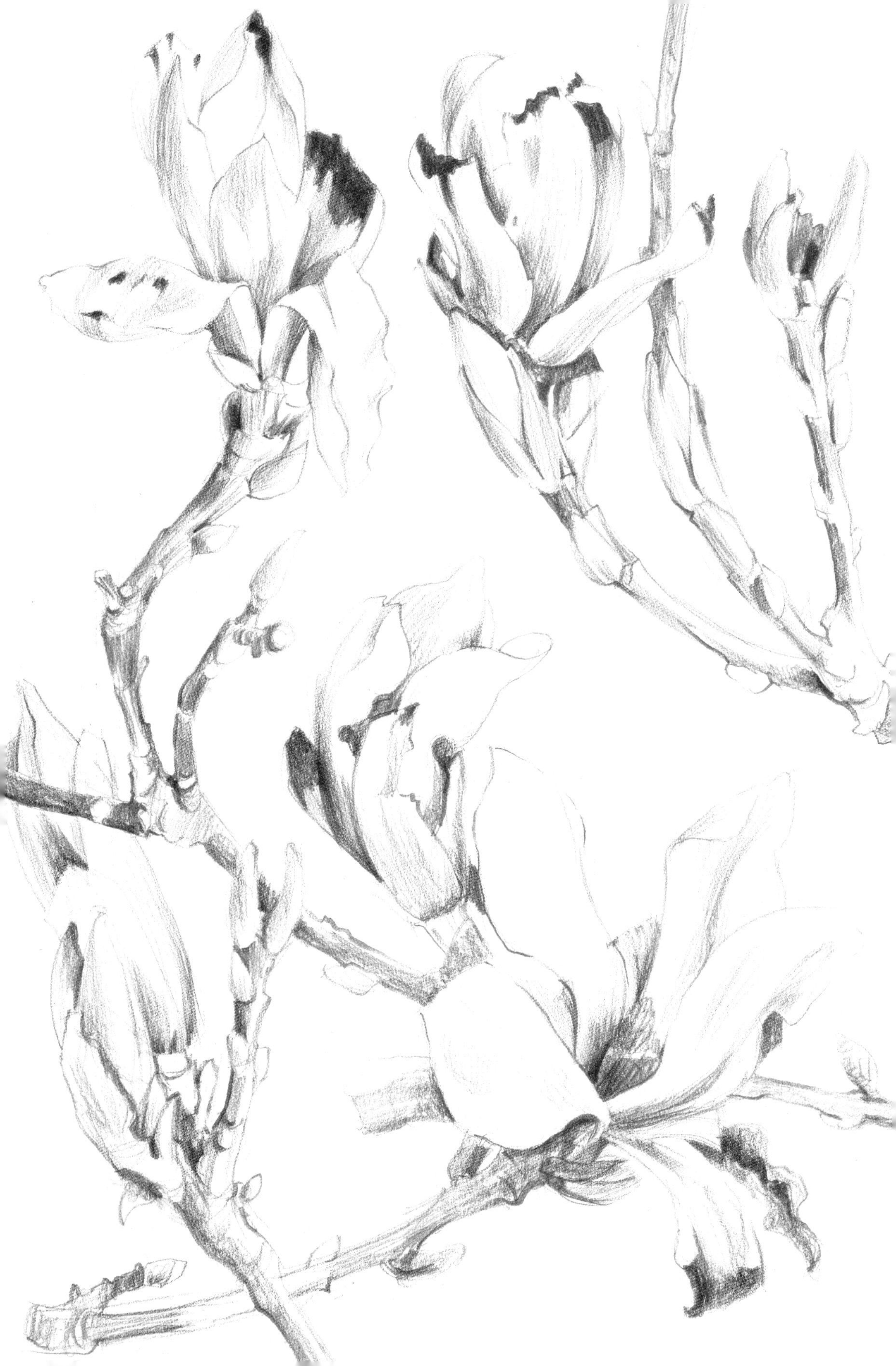

A Frosted Magnolia

Magnolia, so rash although so old
Tempted by the mild and dripping air
Lets its budding flowers escape the fold
Sheds its winter armour for its festive wear.

Real winter upset everything, returned
Thrusting a spear, shiny with a frosty edge.
Only the small birds dodged away and learned
To shelter in some brown and rustling hedge.

Not the magnolia - it could not wait and did not know
What stratagems would hold its banner high
Burst out, ignoring frost and hint of snow
Those white petals naked to the sky.

That sharp and mindless spear, it cut them off
Turned the creamy torches to a sodden grey
A little ice showing on the drinking trough
Enough to mark the ending of their day.

An Easter resurrection brought them back
Turning aside the spear that winter hurled
As browning petals fell upon the track
An ancient glory burst upon the world.

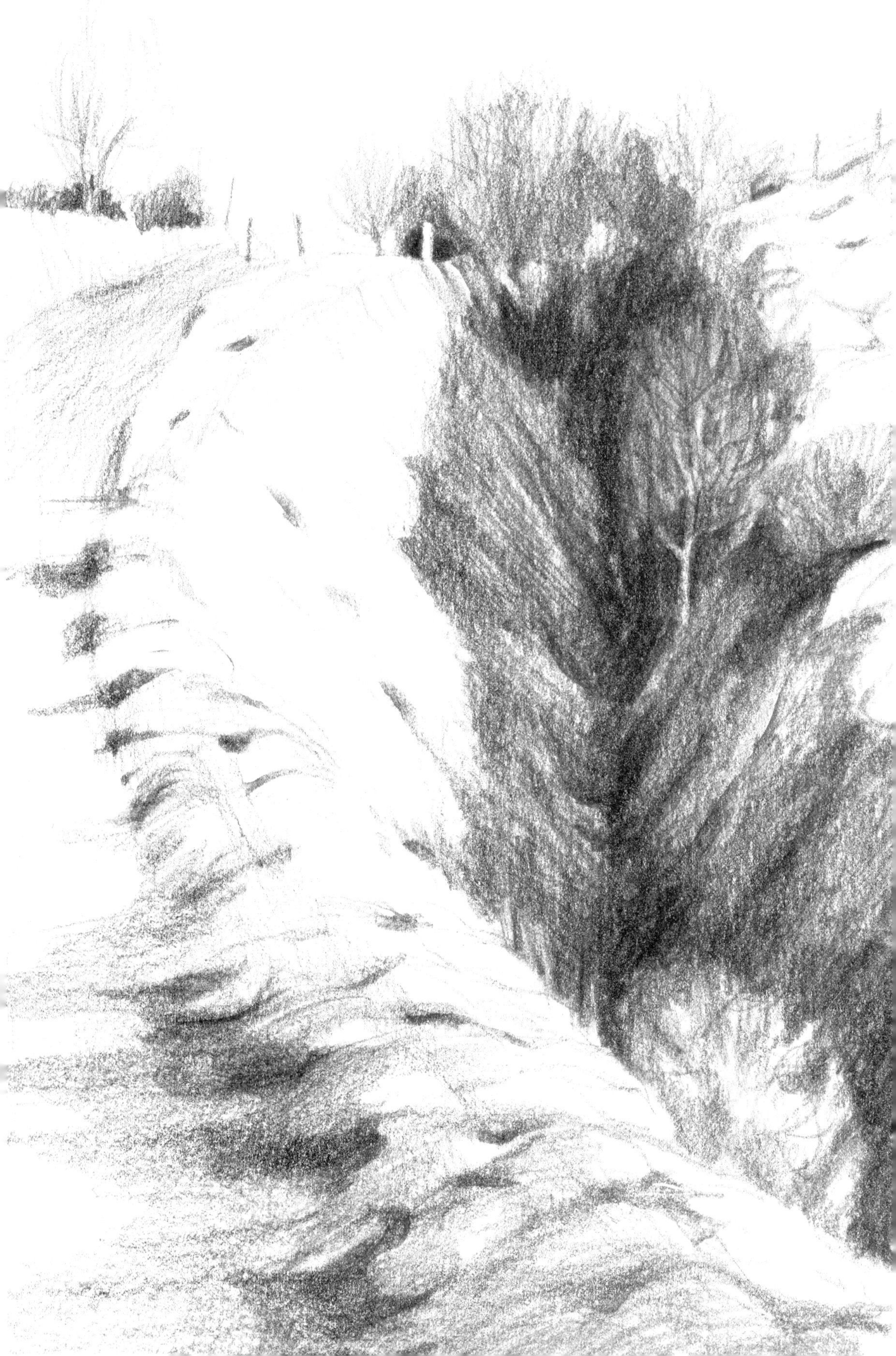

A Walk on Breeze Hill

Why are you walking these hills, old man,
Where the winds blow cold and the clouds lour,
What has pulled you up through the Zig-Zag copse
To the downland which stretches for ever and ever?

Things are not as they were, old man
That shining scene you loved thirty years ago.
Then you watched the hares as they hid and leapt,
In a mad March dance of high and low.

The skylarks now sing somewhere else, old man
Here it's the rooks in the infinite sky,
And the buzzards circling and circling in pairs.
Where the sheep once grazed, the furrows now lie.

You think, old man, you think you remember
The gate to home where once you strode
In that field stretching out like November
Where the lane runs down to the valley road.

It's not there, old man, it's not there
Look further, south-eastwards, and see what you find.
That gate, thank God! Still by the foxes' lair
Then down through the hawthorns you see in your mind.

Will you do it again, old man, again?
The bones creak louder, the night owl calls
Bulbarrow turns dim in sunset and rain
Across the vale, and for you, the light falls.

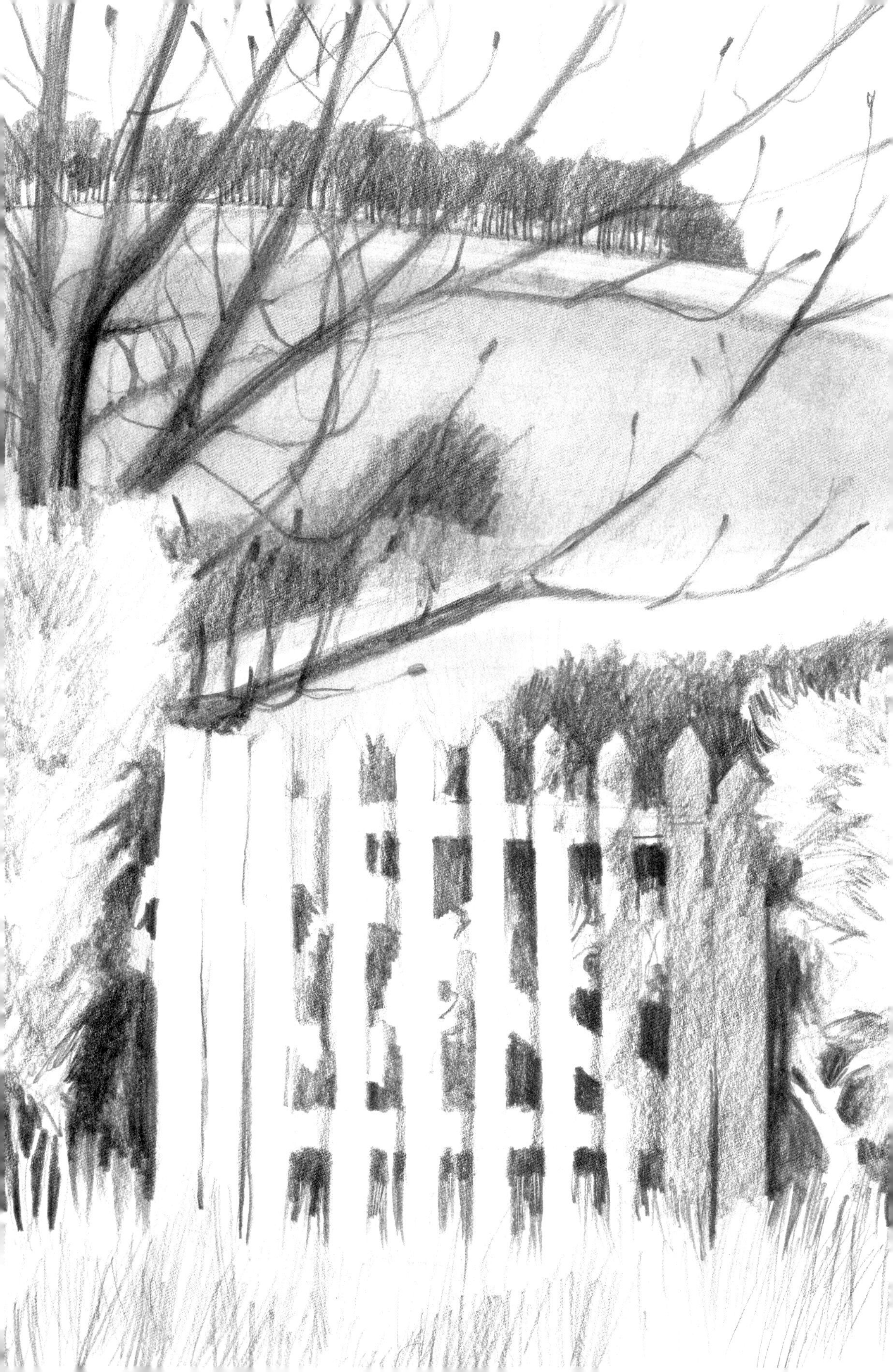

When Samantha Died

Sam the dog died on the kitchen mat
This April evening turning soon to May
The winter garden cold and flat
Hinting only at spring's bloom-spray.

We did not hear or see her die
Held in our own death's imitation
She chose that night a different place to lie
Such an event required a special station.

Sincere, those neighbourly condolences
Wash round our loss with shallow waters
We shrug, denying any resonances
That things go on and nothing alters.

Not so: the tree diminishes though
Only little branches fall
As, alone, I turn back by the farmhouse wall,
Sam does not follow now.

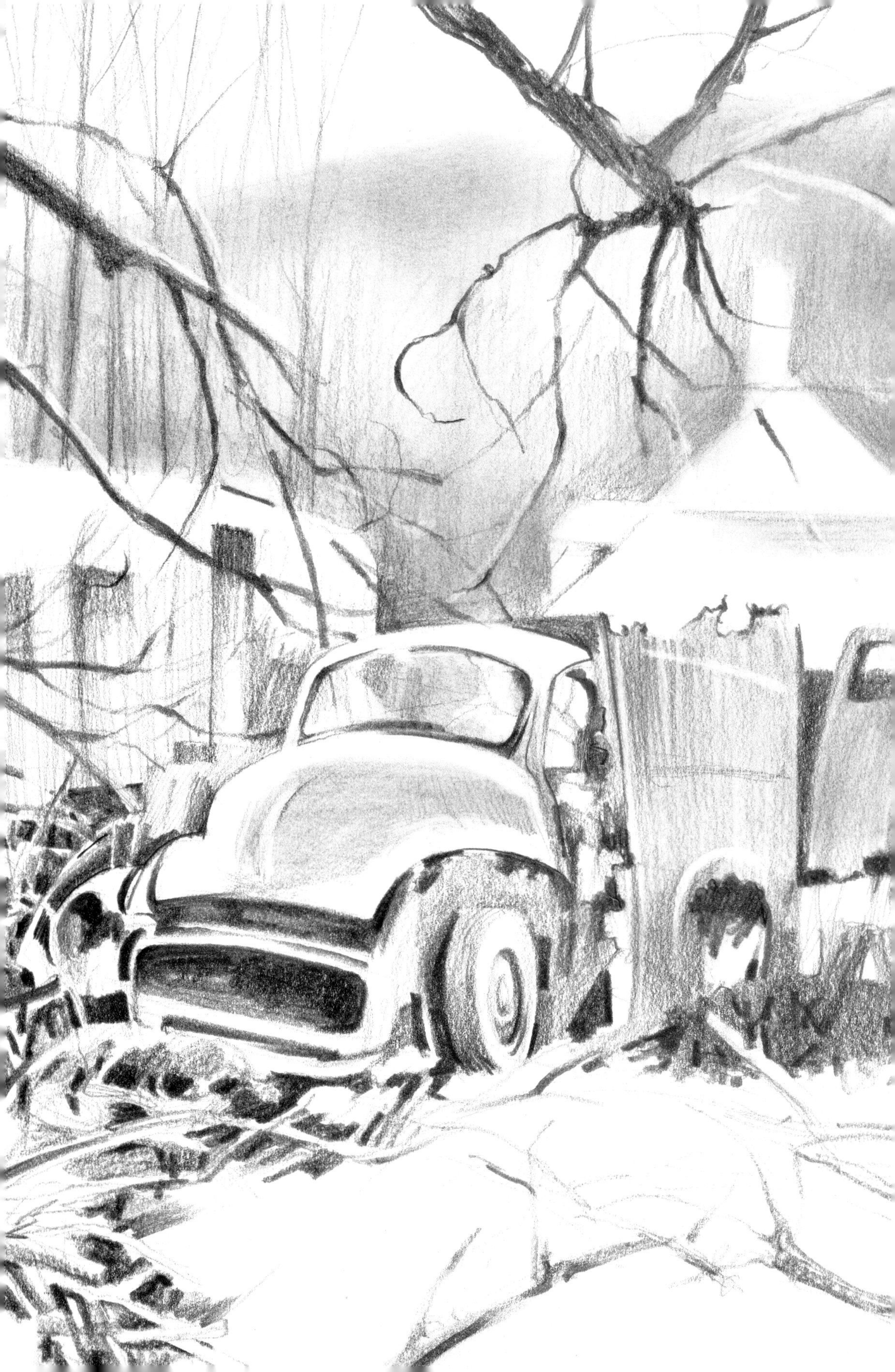

Wincombe Lane: Re-cycling

A Monday morning place, this squared off site
Car service, steel strips and computer store
Men in overalls and women culinary white
Glimpse the sun from factory floor.

For us, Recycling. We who enter there
Waste abandon to its destination
Cardboard, bottles, household and garden pair.
Obedient, we know our proper station.

Into Hell's mouth, the yellow containers
Our morsels, Metal, Plastics, Masonry are tossed
Fragments of our living, those reminders
Of waste and error, hopes dead, chances lost.

But we all grin, comrades in this ditching
Detritus of our melancholy lives,
Such losing, such tossing, is enriching
Start again! now our battered hope revives.

And yet! Though all's correctly placed
With new acquaintances exchange the final quip
We know as well that Household Waste
Is not our final tipping in life's skip.

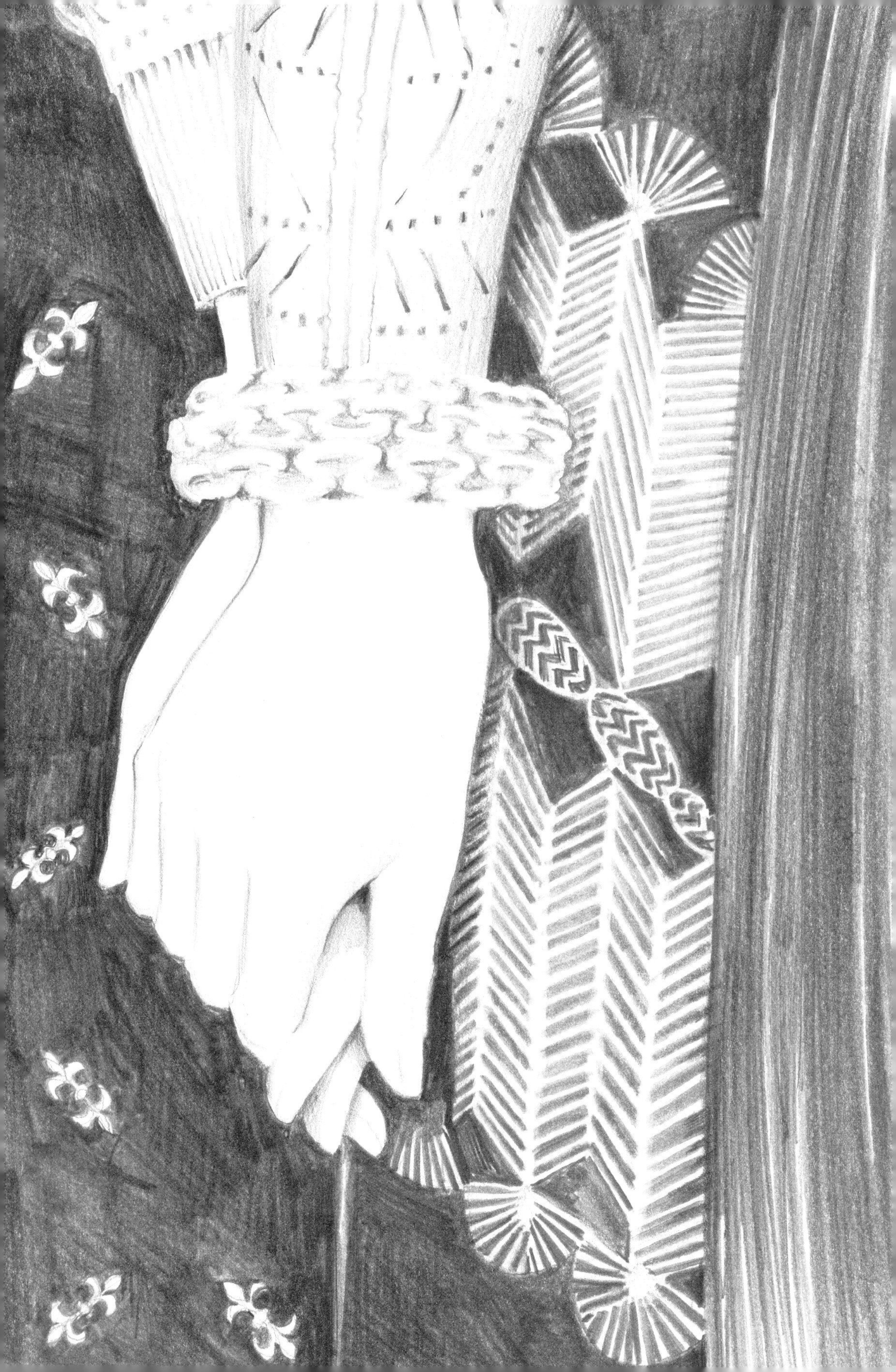

Mozart and Marriage

Struggling to make K332 resemble Mozart
A car door bangs. Visitor lured out by sunny weather?
Outside the big window, a woman in a red hat
Looking at early flowers, aubretia, stylosa and the heather
What was she doing there? Interrupting my arthritic fingers
Defeated by demisemiquavers and irregular B flat.
I see only a shape which stands and lingers.

I know her! How I know her!
For fifty years we have gardened together
Growing love in the long borders of cultivation

Magically, now, it sparks across the air
She leaves the flowers, moving away
Returning through the kitchen door.
Magic, and Mozart, stand aside,
Deferring to our everyday.
All is more wonderful than before.

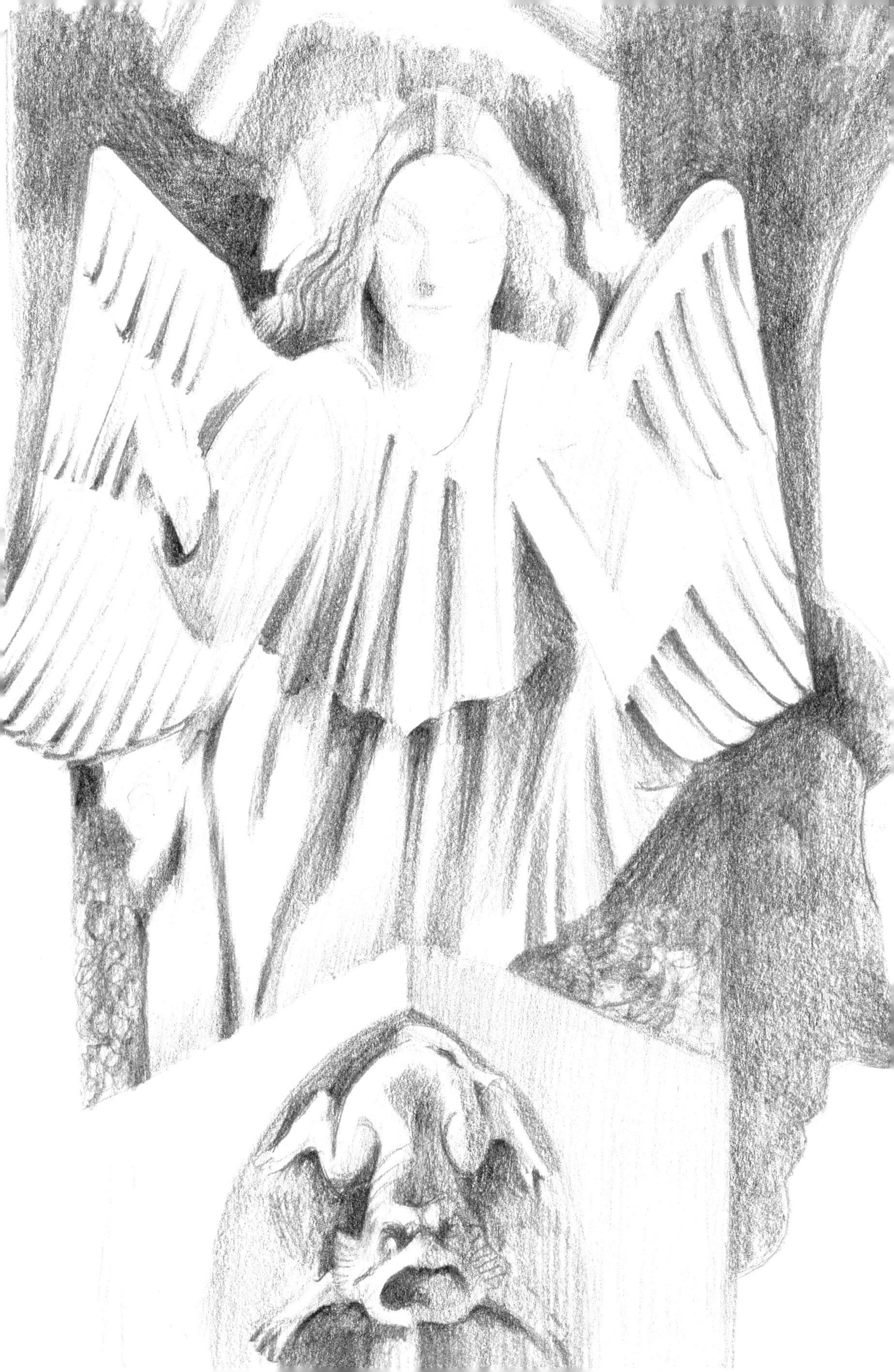

The Future of Daffodils

How do the daffodils come to die?
They danced and danced immortally
In the sunlight where now the fallen catkins lie
Proclaiming Easter day.

Edges curling, decaying from the outside
Where the petals turn into a shroud
Suddenly even the trumpets have died
Cast down the mighty and the proud

Losing eminence, so they lose heart
Tarnished the gold, the silky fabric dank
Tired of the failing the stems fall apart
Lying across the violets on the bank

Was it the bulb still in earth's darkness
Jealous of their trumpeting time out there
Calls them back into the starkness
No longer to toss and flourish in the air?

We see it all with equanimity
Knowing that to feed the bulb the blooms must die
So it has been and will be so again
Certain, we know as April rain.

Suppose, though, useless the toil
The clouds dry
The bulbs dust in a dead soil
Blasted by sun in skies always the same.
A hot season widening out
Turning to one the four of time and our affection
Drying under the universal sun
Lost for ever in the global flame.

Shall we lose our Easter resurrection?

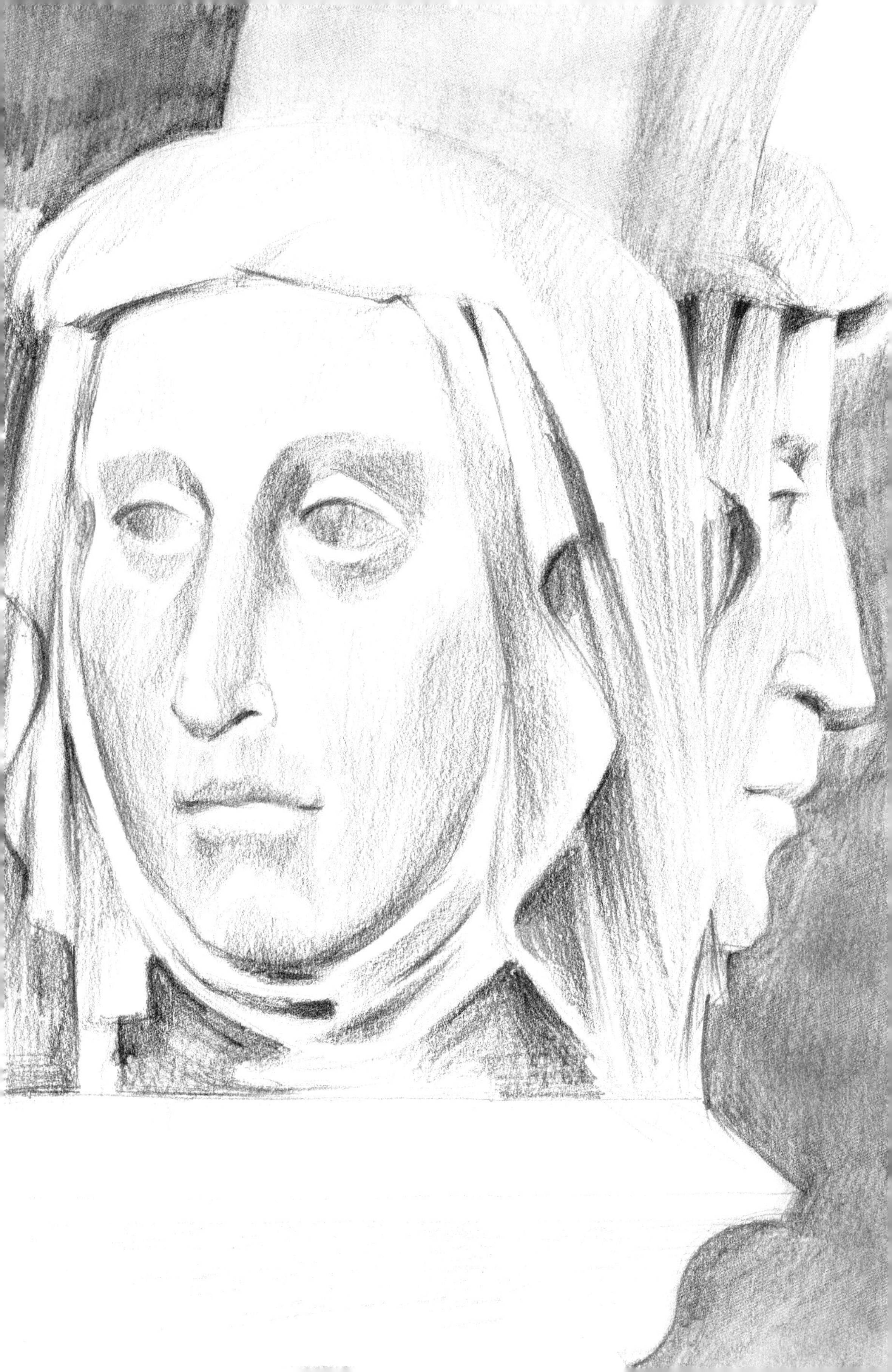

Ash Wednesday: Compline

Half a candle burning in a dark church
The bright east window, the Christian story
Blank since the dying of the morning sun.
A mufti'd priest in a brown pew; across,
An old man wrapped in age and winter's chill.
She speaks low: 'the Lord Almighty grant us
A quiet night and perfect end.' then Paul
Singing his hymn to things of good report.
'Lord, hear our prayer
And let our cry come unto you.'
Will this candle of faith go out as we go now
Into the dark, blank like the east window?

In the lane, looking west to that same church
A tree: ash, ash-grey the gaping trunk
Where near the top two hawks will build a nest.
Who will stop the old tree falling
Where will they go, the nesting sparrow hawks?
Stars emerge and gleam, presaging cold nights.
Far in the West reaching out to Land's End
Cauliflower heads of summit-seeking cloud
Threaten in the western sky.
We have blown out the candle in the church
The sparrow hawks have left the stricken tree
The white clouds soar into infinity.

We know that the candle of faith will burn again
The birds find another nest
In the cloudless skies the stars shine out
' We will lie down in peace and take our rest.'

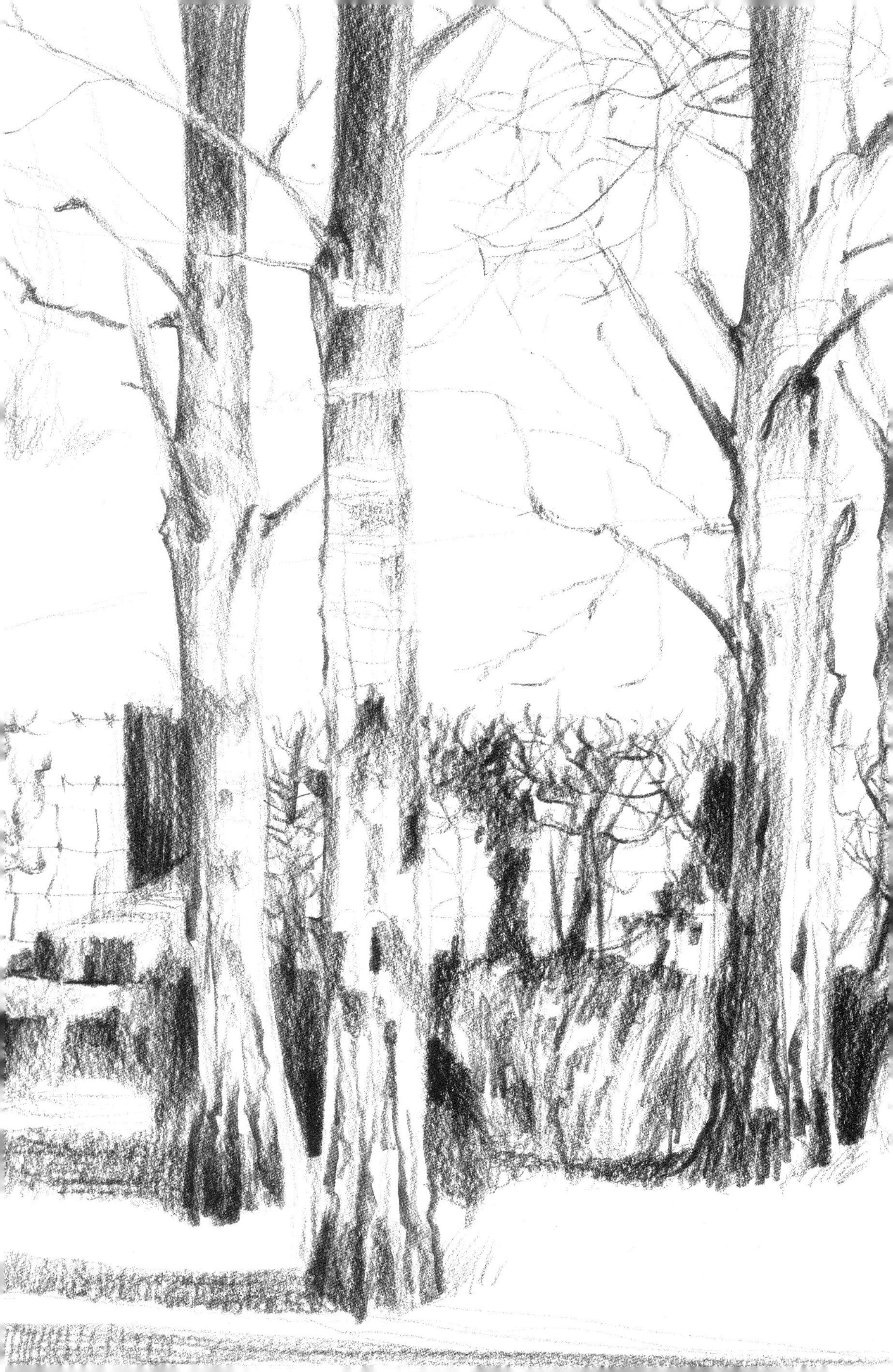

I Shall Walk in my Garden

I shall walk in my garden everyday
Through the arch where the clematis grows
Stand and stare at the spring array
And the springing sprig on the rose.

No-one can tell me, no-one can tell me
Shall I manage to get there tomorrow?
To look again at the black-bud ash tree
For time here you cannot borrow.

The daffodils nod me a greeting
Under the hazel's catkinned spread
Though we and the daffs are but fleeting
Hidden violets waken from dead.

Heathers in purple and hellebores white
Altars for gardens in long Lenten days
Raised from the debris of wintery blight
For offerings of wonder and praise.

The wintering cattle for freedom are lowing
To frolic abroad in the meadow's greens
Beds for the broad beans sighing for sowing
A pheasant strays in and struts as he preens.

Go, oh go, whether raining or fine
Move through the air where the sparrows play
Smile while you can at the pert celandine.
Yes, I shall walk in my garden today.

Hospital, Odstock
Amesbury Ward

The evening sunshine lingers over
Green hedges burgeoning white with may
Small birds sing compline for departing April
Comes the ending of the day.

Now is the time to welcome in relations
Husbands, cousins, children, wives
Nurses murmur at their stations
Healthy ones among those other lives.

Tranquil the ward to match the hour
The fret of day has softened with the sun
Sheet racks shadow the reflecting floor
Patients smile, another day here done.

Yesterday the ward held six, now five
In that short time she lay there gasping dust
With all the hideous trimmings of the kept-alive
Now gone, as golden girls must.

Beyond our ward, others stretch in place,
Holding each its special agonies
Beyond, the many cities, globes and space
Housing each its sad, recurrent, tragedies.

Perhaps, they say, it was a better fate
When folks so sick just stayed at home and died
That all this mighty apparatus which makes death late
Has purpose mainly to sustain our pride

We, the not so bad, the getting better
Count to our release the hopeful hours
Aware that we too are death's debtors
And her fate, surely, will one day be ours.

Whiteparish Ward

Shadows thread through artificial light
Here where we miscellaneous patients lie
An old man pleads to end his year long fight
A shout proclaims his wish to die

Silenced then the murmuring student band
Who trail the suited specialist
Falls to his side his white, expository hand
He has no words for this.

A cure so perfect and complete
Derides all other possibilities
Now medicine accepts defeat
It cannot stand with such infinities.

May Morning

Rejoice in the spring
Chestnut, and May white in a new season
Purged by winter
And the clouds too, only less white
In that bright sky, blowing across the universe,
Make trees and hills mere props
On a small earth stage.

Then the young people,
Helmeted aviators
Braking on bikes
Free of caution and taking off into those clouds
Like our Hugh bursting now through the gate.

We, quiescent in these moving landscapes
Regain too our innocence,
Eliminate loss, sorrows and mistakes
Looking up through the chestnut trees.

Suddenly it seems, rain falls, driven by winds invisible,
Shaking the white trees, greying the clouds
Aviators racing home, Hugh going
Leaves torn from the trees.
We stay, losing that fleeting innocence with the broken sky,
Lost in a violent world
Where May petals fall with the rain.

SUMMER

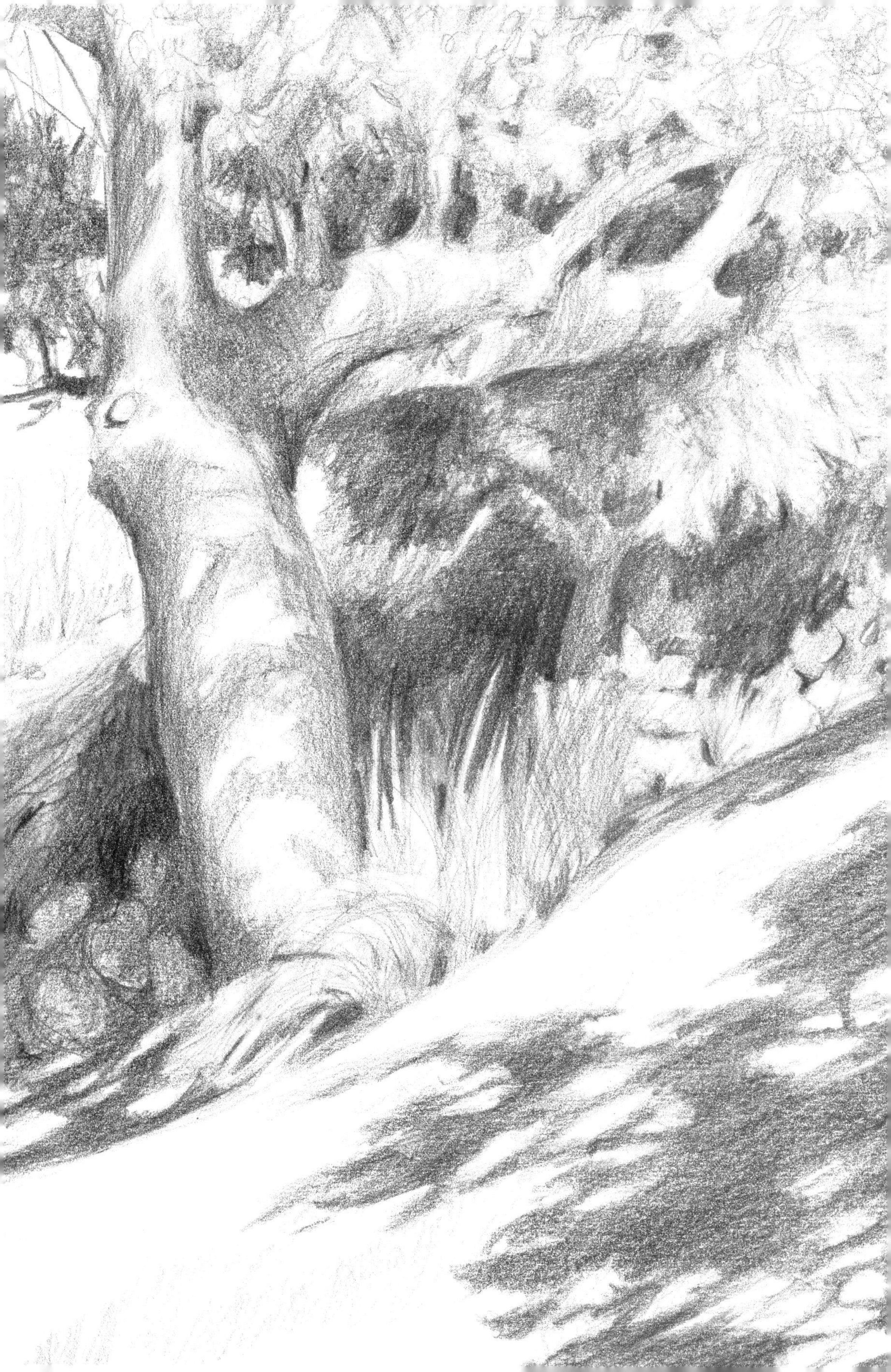

June Walk

Through a garden where yellow yields to blue
Blues then to reds.
Across the plank to fields
Held in the hand of the great hills.
Southerly, newly done, a brown ploughed square
Abstract, seeming for ever.
All this, the first of summer, the best.

June is the freshest and the loveliest month
Of all our summer joys.
Now, now is the moment!
Winds turn new grasses into waves
Flowing with measured pace towards the deeper green
Of older fields, recalling shores of estuaries.
I sail this dancing sea, driven by a billowing shirt
Through green and green again
Affront the mighty wave of steep Breeze Hill
Crested with hawthorn bloom, a breaking foam.
Butter-coloured Devons stand and graze
Rooted beneath the blue, blue cap of sky.

Not just, in June, the green, the blue the brown the white
There's gentle golden loveliest light
To wrap around the meaning of each day
Alas! How brief its stay.

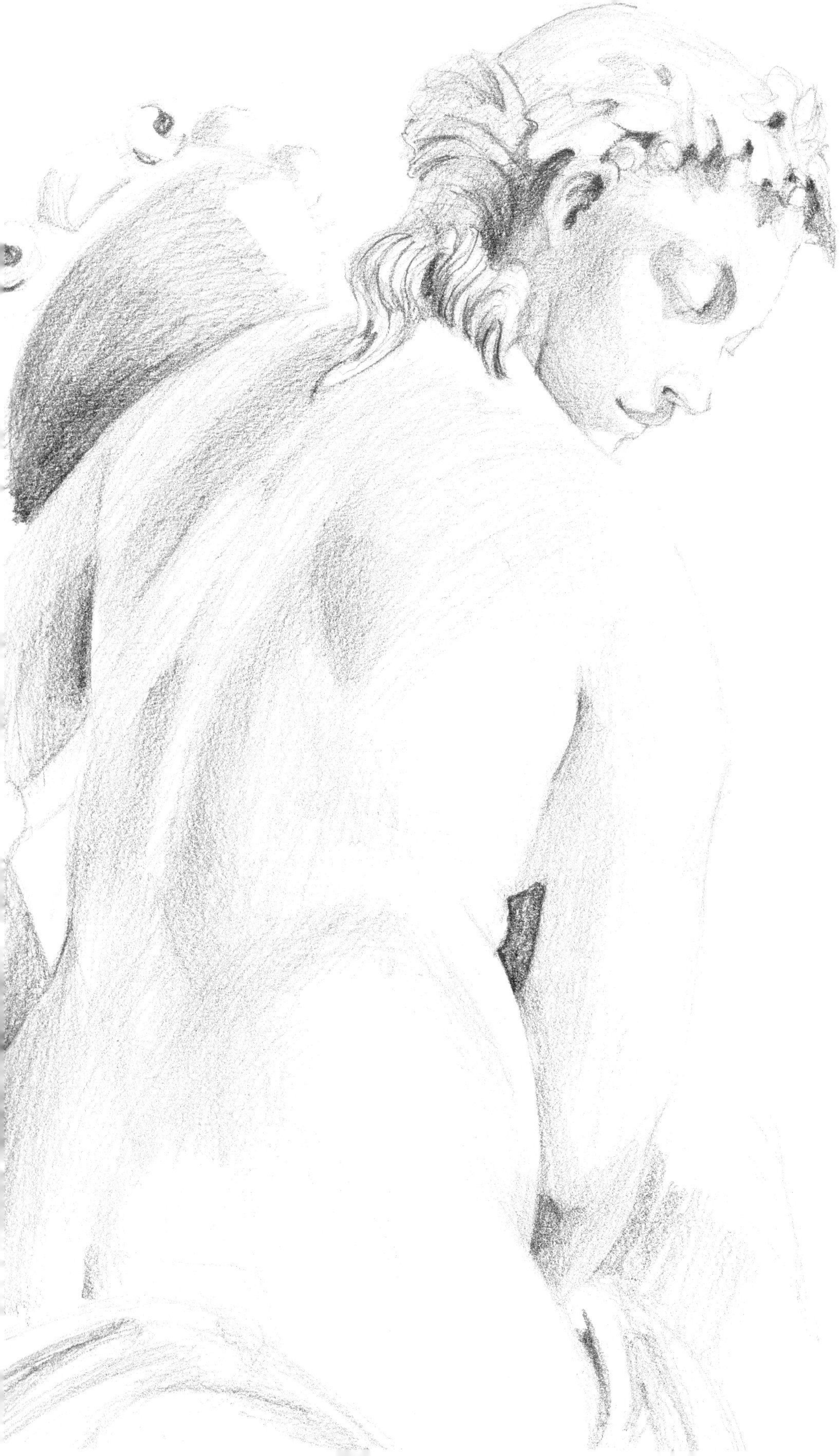

Concert, Port Regis

The promise of such music called her up
From the lake beyond the window
To the stool beside the grand.
She turns the pages, this fair river-girl
Hair falling to creamed breasts
Her jeans are made to thresh through water
Now her limbs are still.

Poulenc's scream of pain
Against that Spanish war
Transforms the fiddler to a sheet of light
Glittering like the lake
Where other river-girls dwell.

Music ends, she leaves, into the lake
Sliding silently, mysteriously, out of our air.
Pianist and fiddler bow and surf applause.

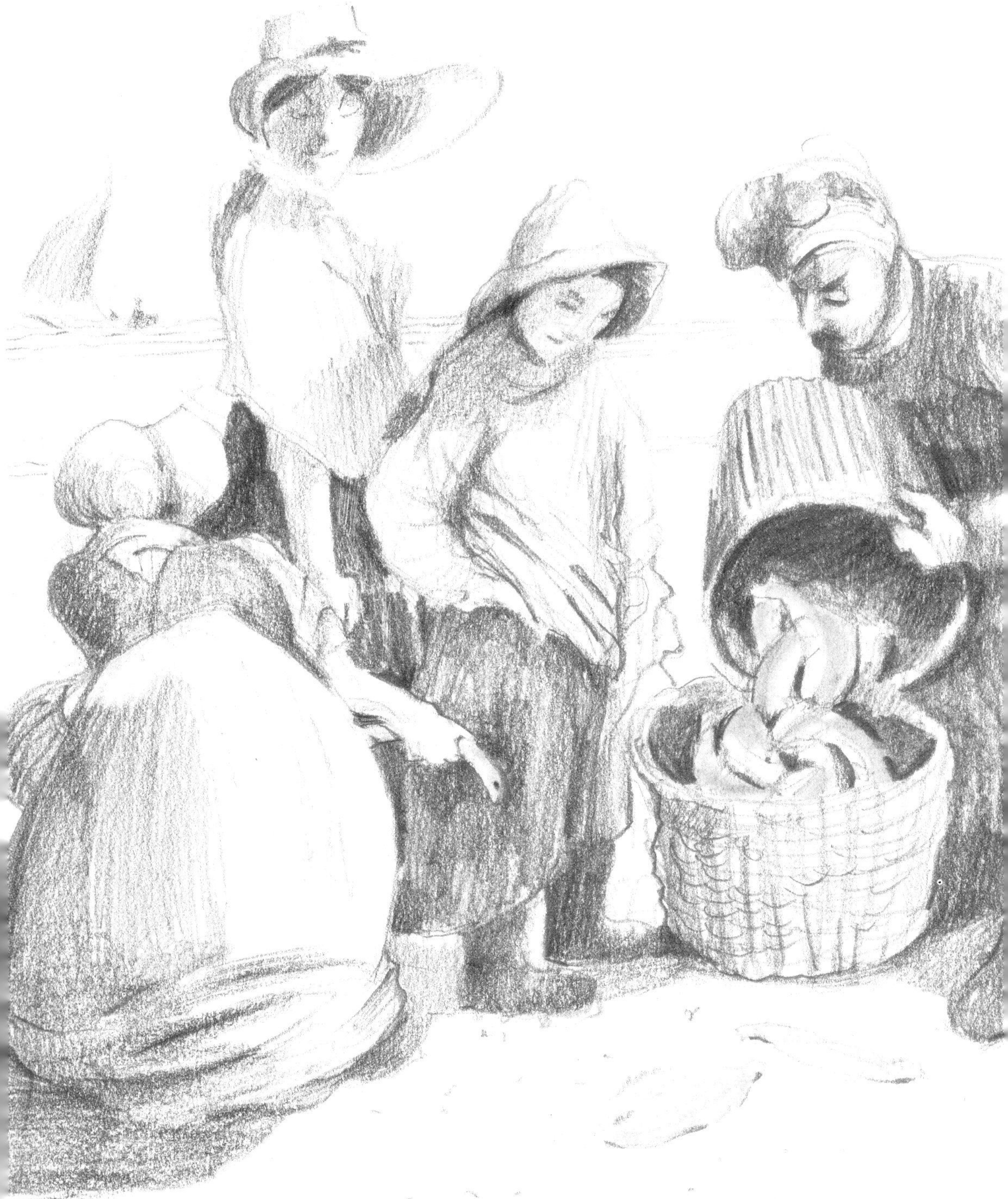

Tennyson Down

Sea - the sun dances all over you
Not one colour, plenty,
Blue, but that won't do
You've got twenty.

That sun is your girl
Rising, setting, with rare constancy
You, sea - shifting-shifty, deep-deceitful, all a swirl
She should know your mendacity.

You do well against us, human men
We'd drown and you'd not care
Much too much of you, southwards no end
So I stay here, in that old poet's lair.

You're just water, water everywhere, H_2O
No mind, no body, no soul.

New House in the Lane

Around the year we all complain,
That new house dumped across the road
Far too big to suit a little lane
Outstrips the one assigned to God.

Too many windows, countless gables
It cuts a scar across the green
Too many garages, too many stables
Stuck upon this gentle scene.

Then, this morning, topping the hedges
The early sunshine caught the chimney stack
Held in its rays the soft stone edges
The corners throw the shadows back

No longer harsh and overweight
A simple, perfect, glowing stone
Delicately tops that roof of slate
And makes a mansion home.

Not a great event - a simple perfect sight
Sun, hedge, stack, never again
So framed, transfixed by such a light.
Restored, that moment, the wholeness of the lane.

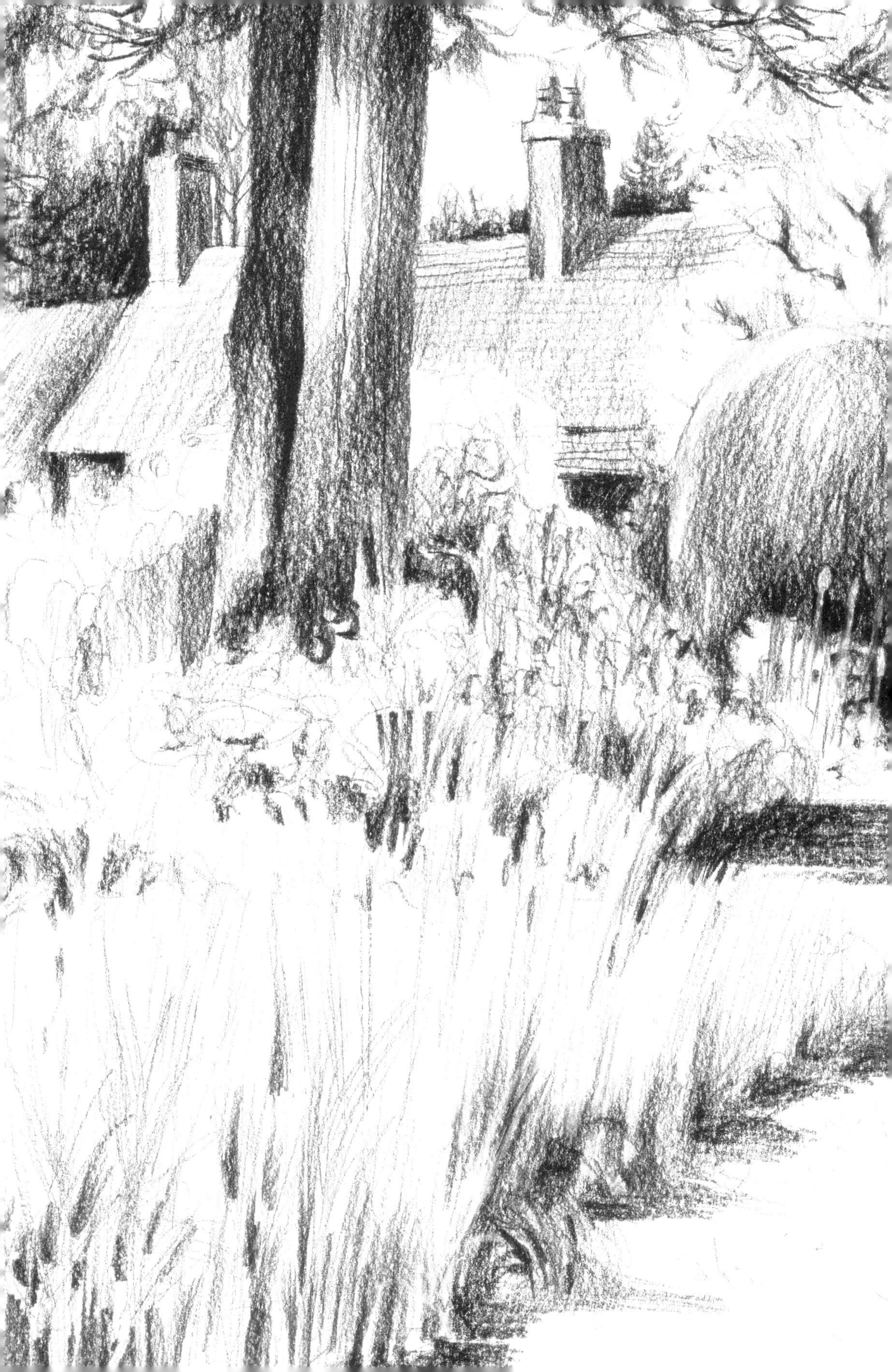

At an Exhibition: Iris Stylosa

The greensand house built before the Abbey fell
Aging to a beauty greater than its merchants knew
Who heard the murmurings of prayer beyond the wall
And Compline sung upon the evening air.
In the garden, by the wall, a plant
Dispirited by rain and wind, iris stylosa.
In the exhibition, perfect; on white paper
A flame in spaces of pure light.
Here live the artists
Made merry by music and the south-west winds.

Beyond, the other worlds
Where bored policemen hang about
Grinding through routines
To guard the exploded, fragmented buses
While footballers rampage
In the engulfing stadiums.
Over global horizons, the ethnic slaughterers roar
Typhoons ride the flooding lowlands
While mountains splinter and tectonic plates
Crash to drive the great waves.

What must they do, what must they do, those other inhabitants?
How will they wander through many rooms
Sit under the fruited trees
Calm on lawns trailed by the moon?
Will they paint their iris stylosa
Hair lofted by the winds
To the sounds of clarinets?

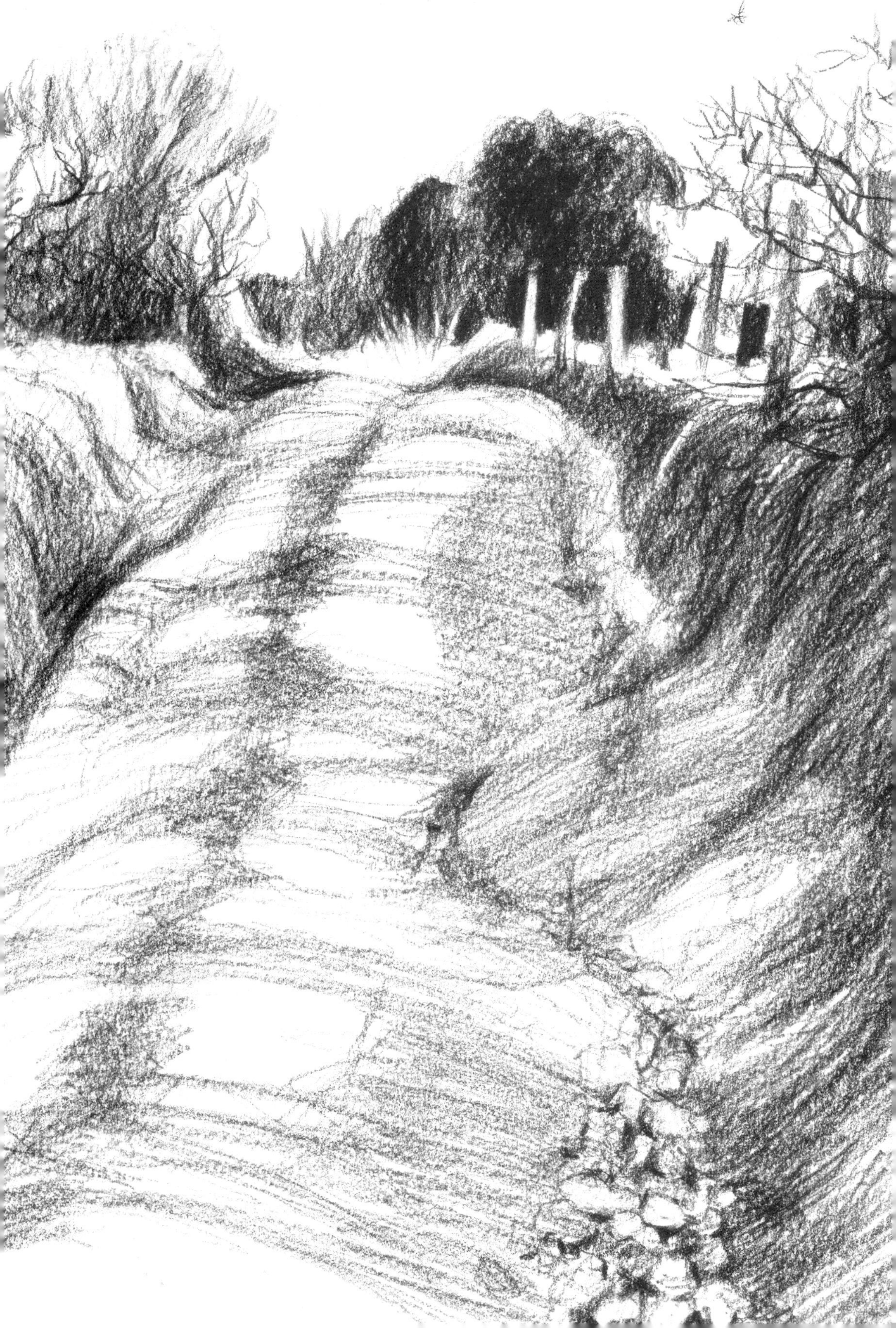

Westminster Hospital Shaftesbury

3pm: the sterile middle of all afternoons,
The stale of August lingering still.
These walls invade green space
Which hangs from Abbey gate to Melbury hill.

Inside you see the old folk shuffle as they make
Their way by turn to the indifferent hall
Claim presence only with the space they take
Wait in a gentle murmur for their call.

That grey hair lovely as her earlier gold
Grown then in wild profusion
Now tamed to suit the state of being old
Frame blue eyes shadowed by confusion.

Beyond, a wheelchair in the window bay,
He sits by walls and spaces which no vistas give
Does not answer, has no words to say
We cannot understand these silent lives.

To this sealed world of corridors and ward
From roaring towns the hustling nurses come
Breathing another air beneath another sun.
He twitches with faint memories of home.

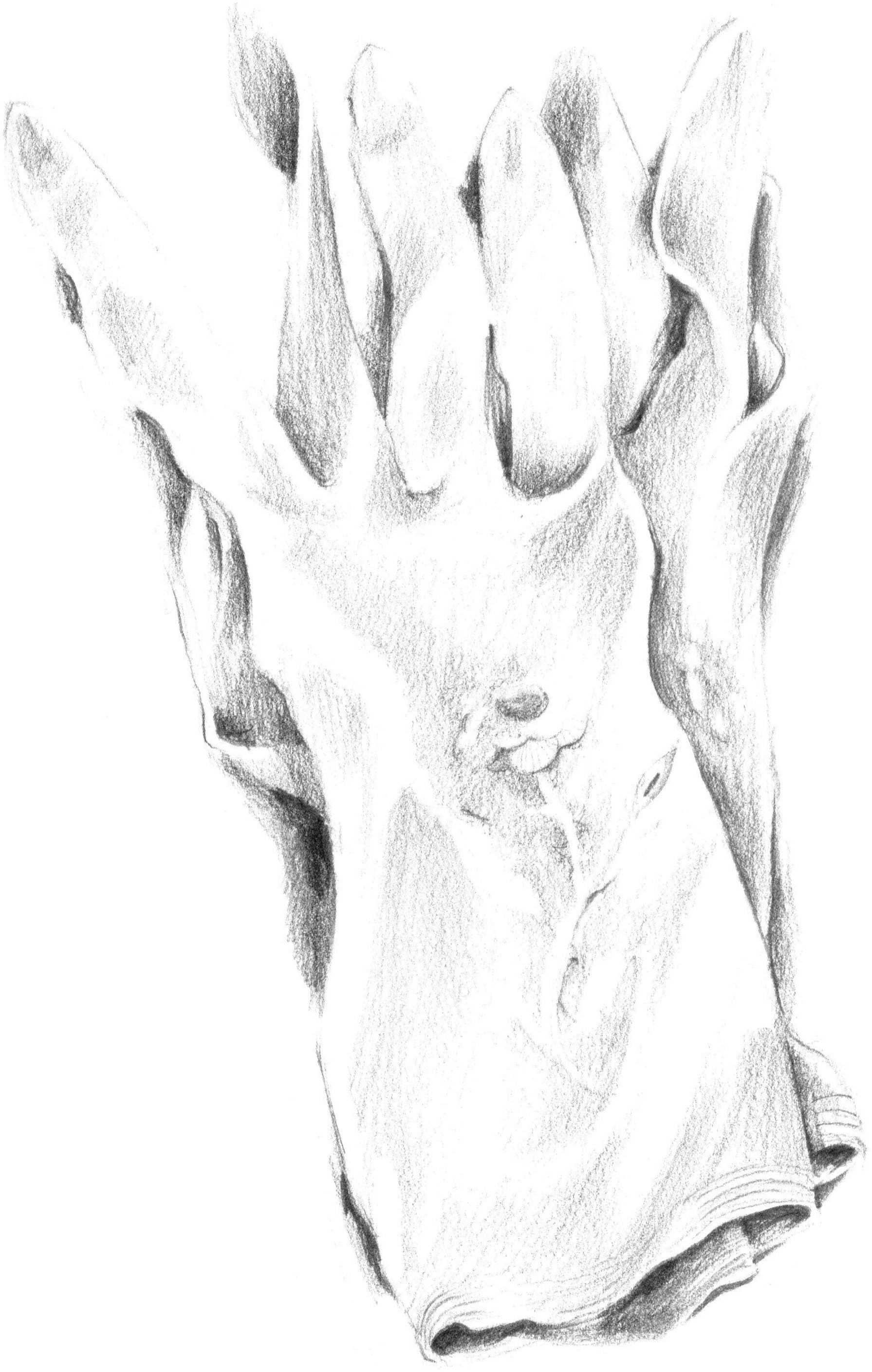

A Rose Song

About my rose, sad Schubert might have writ a song
Surviving winter though so small
Nurtured and loved by people it grew strong
Frost, winds and deluge it defied them all.

In a cold spring, the bush stayed ringed with weeds
Till, in the rising year a warm night
And one morning's sun, the hidden petals feed
Till bud becomes a smouldering red light.

August's bloom, its destiny the village prize,
A beauty, patrician mid peasant bean and pea.
God-made colour, foliage and size
A tune torn from edges of eternity

Fortissimo - a crashing dissonance
Gales blow pools of petals on the lawn
Schubert offers some sad recompense
That tune returns, soaring through the damp dawn.

There's no cosmic lesson to be learnt and said
From Schubert's anguish and this rain
Just petals soaked a dimmer red
And one immortal melody of pain.

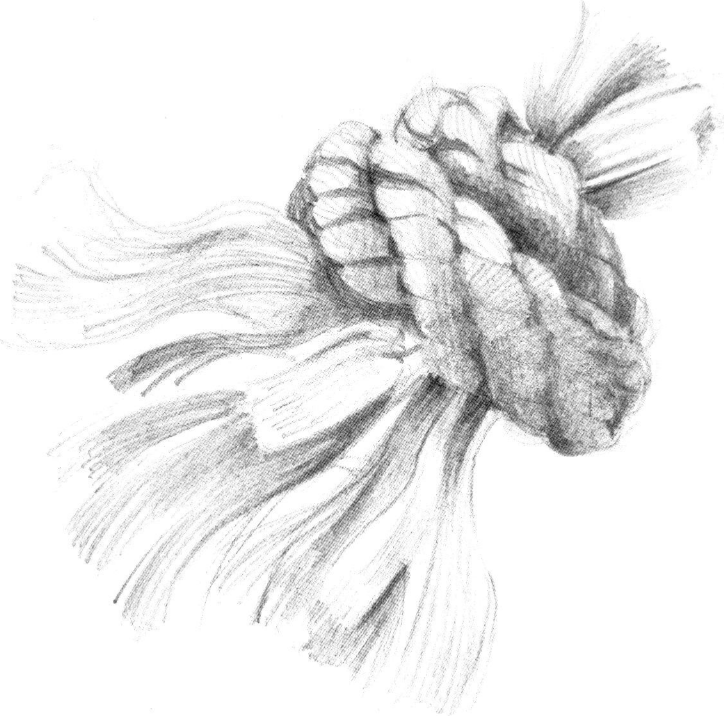

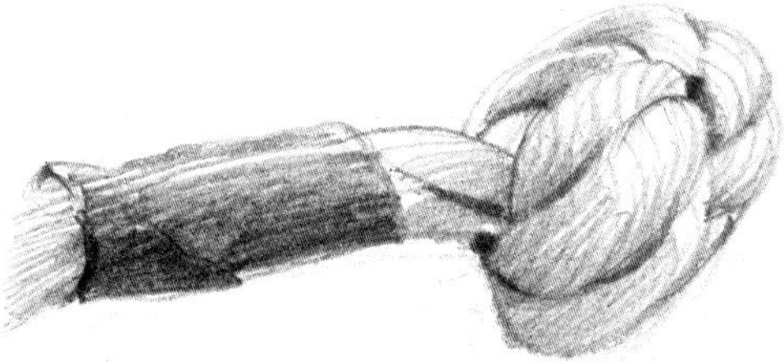

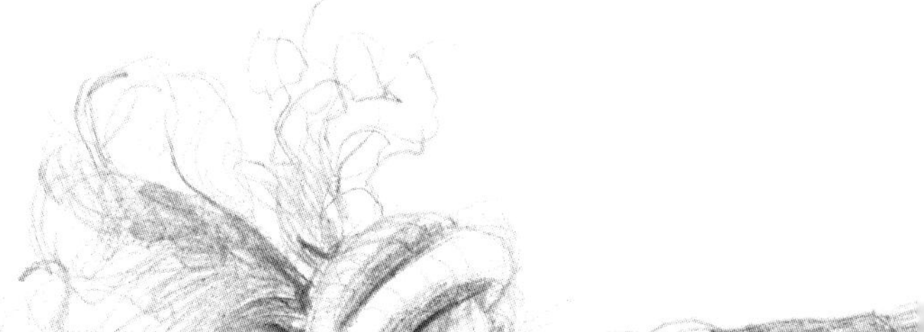

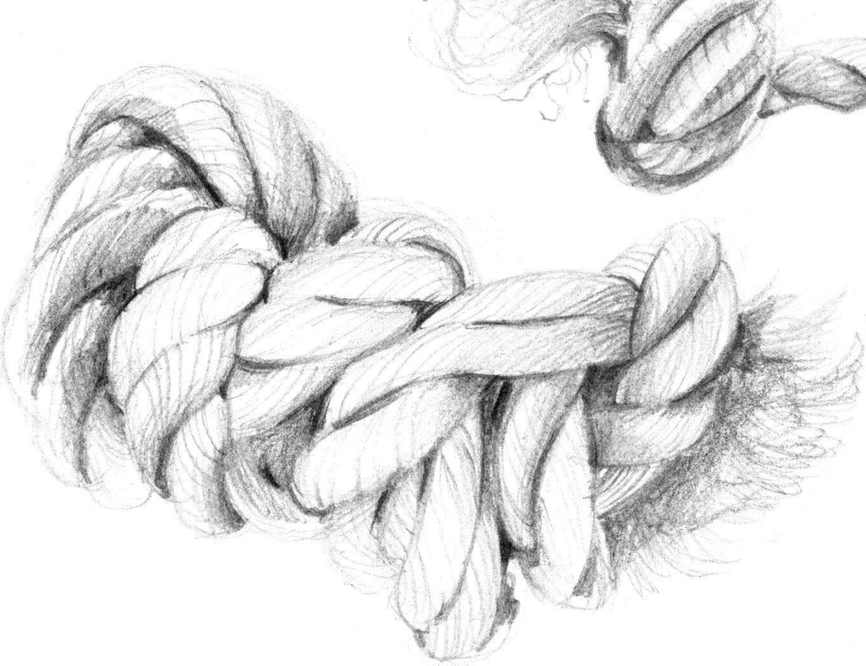

Committee

Like a flute his voice lays out his fears,
Long prepared for this committee day
Words roll : criteria, meaningful, peers
Form squares and march away.

Old men suck and smile behind their teeth
Thinking of eagles sunk on council courses
Recall dawn rides upon the heath
Seeing again a silhouette of horses.

Fingers betray them; the clasped hand
Noses caressed, heads propped
Lips are picked and pleasures planned
Assume, though old, that hearts will beat unstopped.

Chairmen, agendas, minutes, motions
' All go swiftly into the dark'
Medicines, drugs, pills and potions,
Keep committee to the mark.

Rage is concealed by smooth exteriors,
Torments ferment beneath the skin
Arthritis stabs at thin posteriors.
Members speak morality and think of sin.

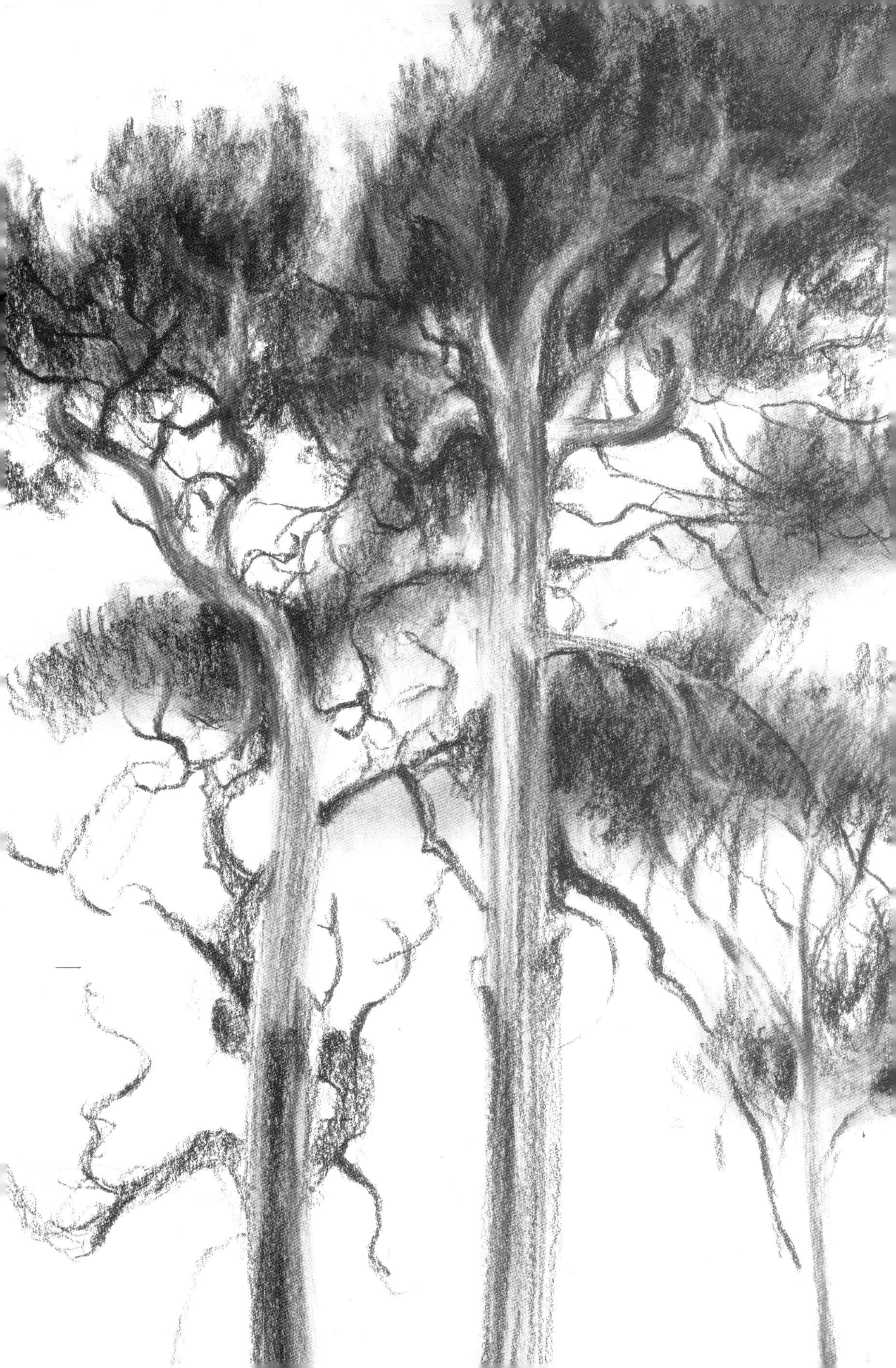

Golden Wedding

Poets continually sing of love
Passion, possession, devotion and delight
Compare their wooing to the cooing of the doves
When love's ignored, lament their plight.

None sings of marriage, its murmuring themes
Its details carried over week by week
There, hid in the repetition of routines,
Lies a diamond far too tough to break.

Come then, you poets, compare us to the seasons
Summer, yes, but lovely winter too
Say that through the fog of human reasons
For us as well love stays as true.

So, please, of marriage sing,
Quietly, sweetly set out its joys
Disturb not the peace within its golden ring
Sweet silence in a world of noise.

AUTUMN

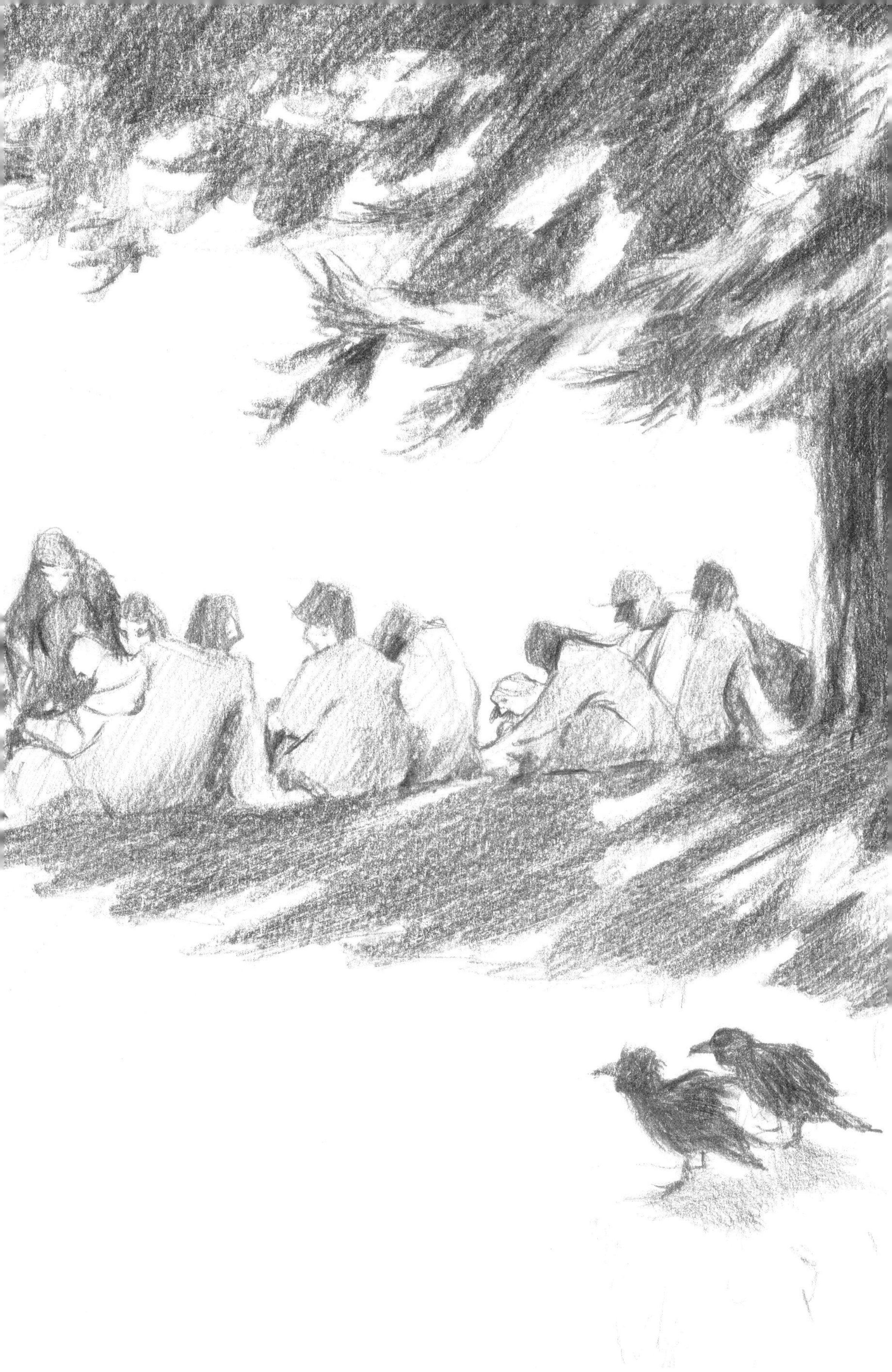

End of Summer

Tea drains from our cup, leaving a stain
A wine drop clings inside a goblet
The mower does not cut the plantain
In the dark garden a faint light lingers yet.

Grandchildren leave as school insistent calls
Dump the riotous jumble by the bed.
Flung aside the stumps, the bat, the balls
Chucked in the silent garden shed.

For us no silence, the memories ring
With cries, the crying and the laughter
Of summer they continually sing
We strive to fix them in the ear.

This is not the way they hear or see
Only the present is the potent.
We hear voices in the wind-rustled tree
And strive to hold the affectionate moment.

We cannot - keep only the teacup stain and goblet drop
Unreal children lost beyond this context
Dusty in that mislaid snapshot
Who shall we see when they come next?

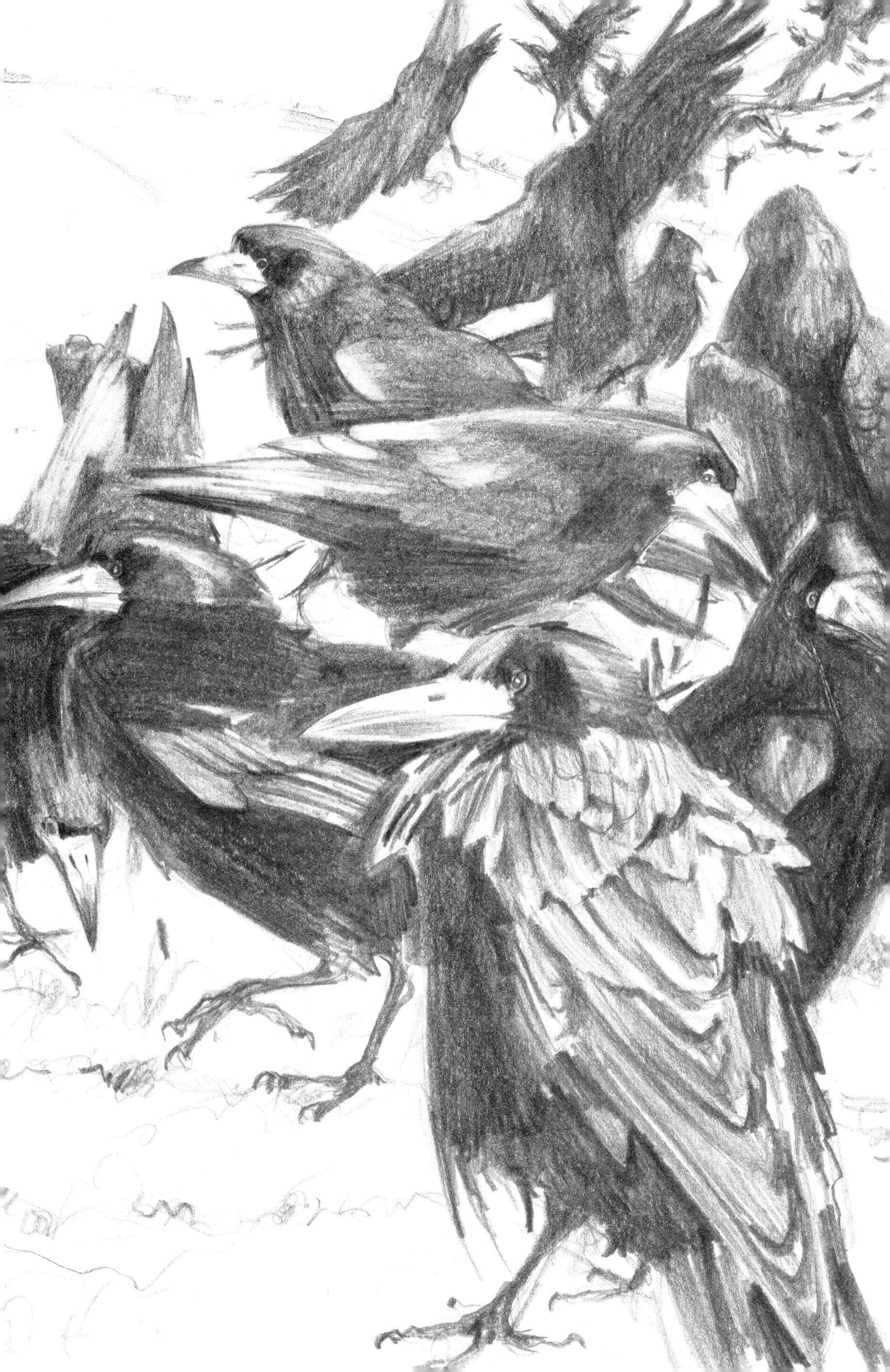

A Hundred Crows

From Horse Ground field they rise as one
Spread in two exploding circles in the sky
No human reason - no fox, no dog, no gun
That I hear. Inspired, they just fly.

Round and upward till the leader stalls
All haloed briefly in late summer's glow
It fades gently as the light falls
In the ash tree now, densely squat those crows.

We despise them, we say ' old crows'
But in flight! Riding the west wind, swirling down
In typhonic descents. Moving in air, highs, lows
Climbing mountains of it, tumbling round and round.

Now in chaotic crowds they fly against grey
Skies and over darkening fields
There they counterpoint black Angus pulling hay
From fodder racks.
Suddenly, unseen, the hundred crows have gone.

Where have they gone? Why are they there?
Flying for ever in the endless air?

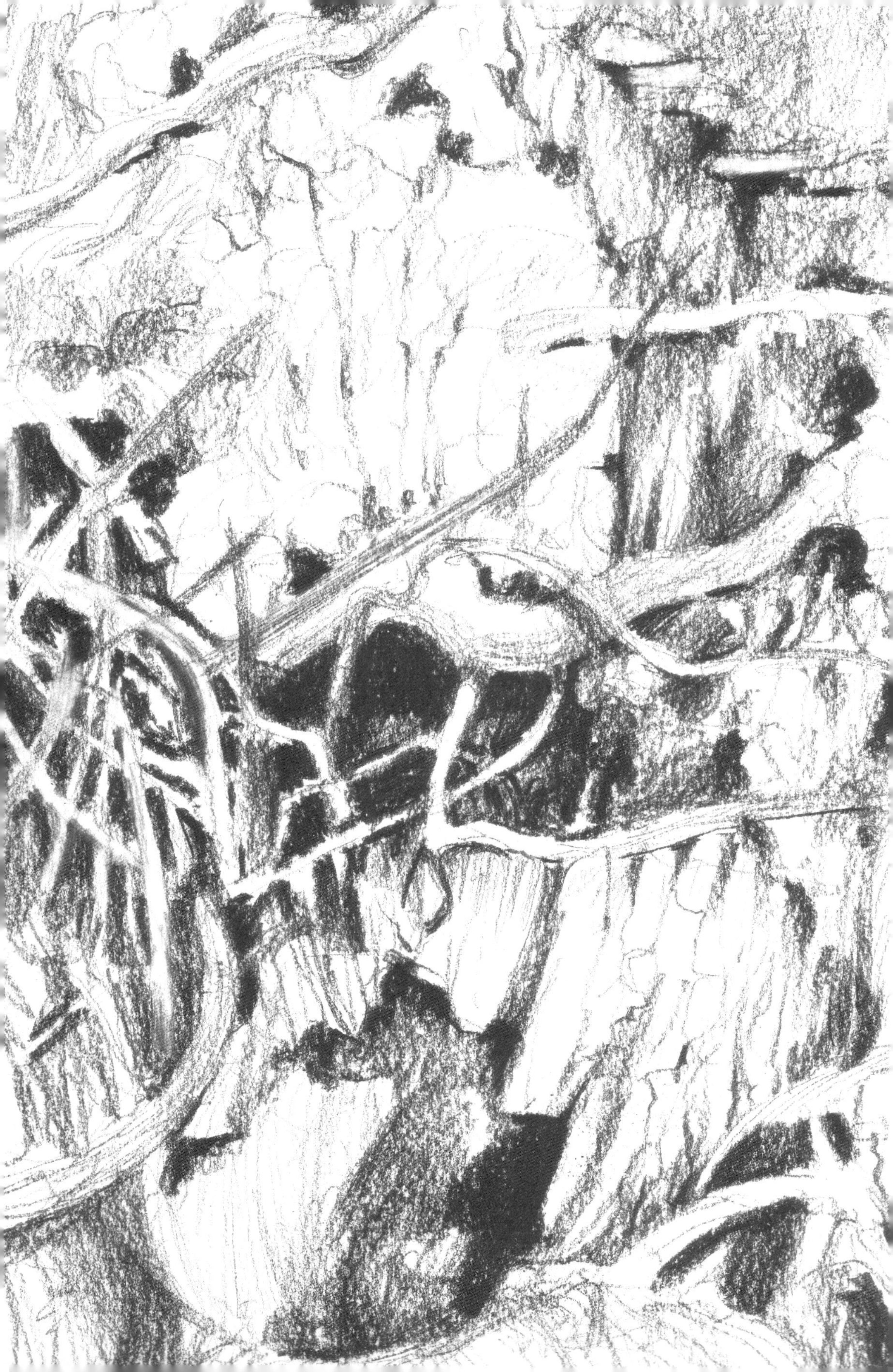

In the Lane

An old man in an older lane,
Held in autumn's falling sun
The wind sweeps up the summer's dust
It rests by the gate where the badgers run.

Wavers and wobbles, the little old bitch
Replica of our decrepitudes
Sniffs in inquisition of the ditch
Tires quickly, pees slowly, turns home.

This garden illustrates the melancholy tale
Sorbus lutescens, spring's olived silver, dead;
The stems snap in final, sharp derision
Of the expectant axe-head, grinning in the shed.

Perhaps, no use to say as poets do,
That winter comes, and spring's not far behind
Will that be so for man and dog. these two ?
Just as well 'the answer's blowing in the wind.'

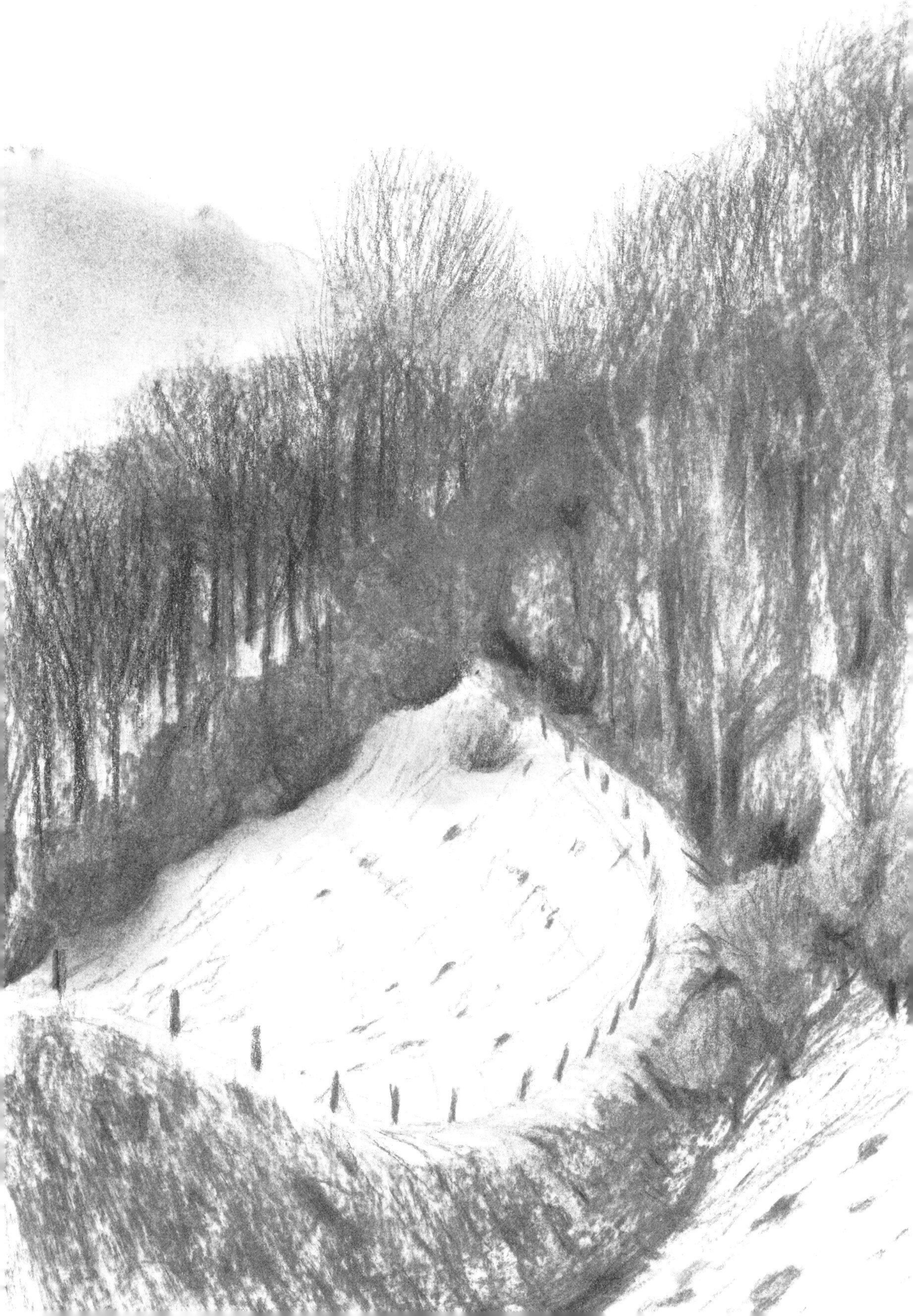

An Autumn Walk

I walk the field below the fall of Zig-Zag hill
Pushed by a south wind
Clouds race the sun to occupy blue space
And light or dim the world.
Affront my halting stick an ever moving band
Of warmth that I must reach
Teases; as I set my foot upon the edge
Clouds catch the sun and I grow cold.
In the stubble left by the yellow, bellowing monster,
A black streak on the chequer board
Of green and golden fields,
My eighty years a field of stubble
An average sort of crop
Warmth now gained, now lost
Fitfully in the sun.

The field ends, blocked by high hedges
Nothing visible beyond.
Turning back, the cloud and sun rush over me
Racing to the road
Wiltshire behind, all Dorset south
Reaching to the unseen sea.
The north downs flatten Charlton way
Breeze hill folds round to Compton down
To Melbury Beacon.
Beneath such hills our house lies low.

As evening falls, the sun, victor of the skies
Drives the clouds beyond horizons
Then also sinks to leave the world cold
While fieldfares play their quidditch still.
Homeward I race the dark.

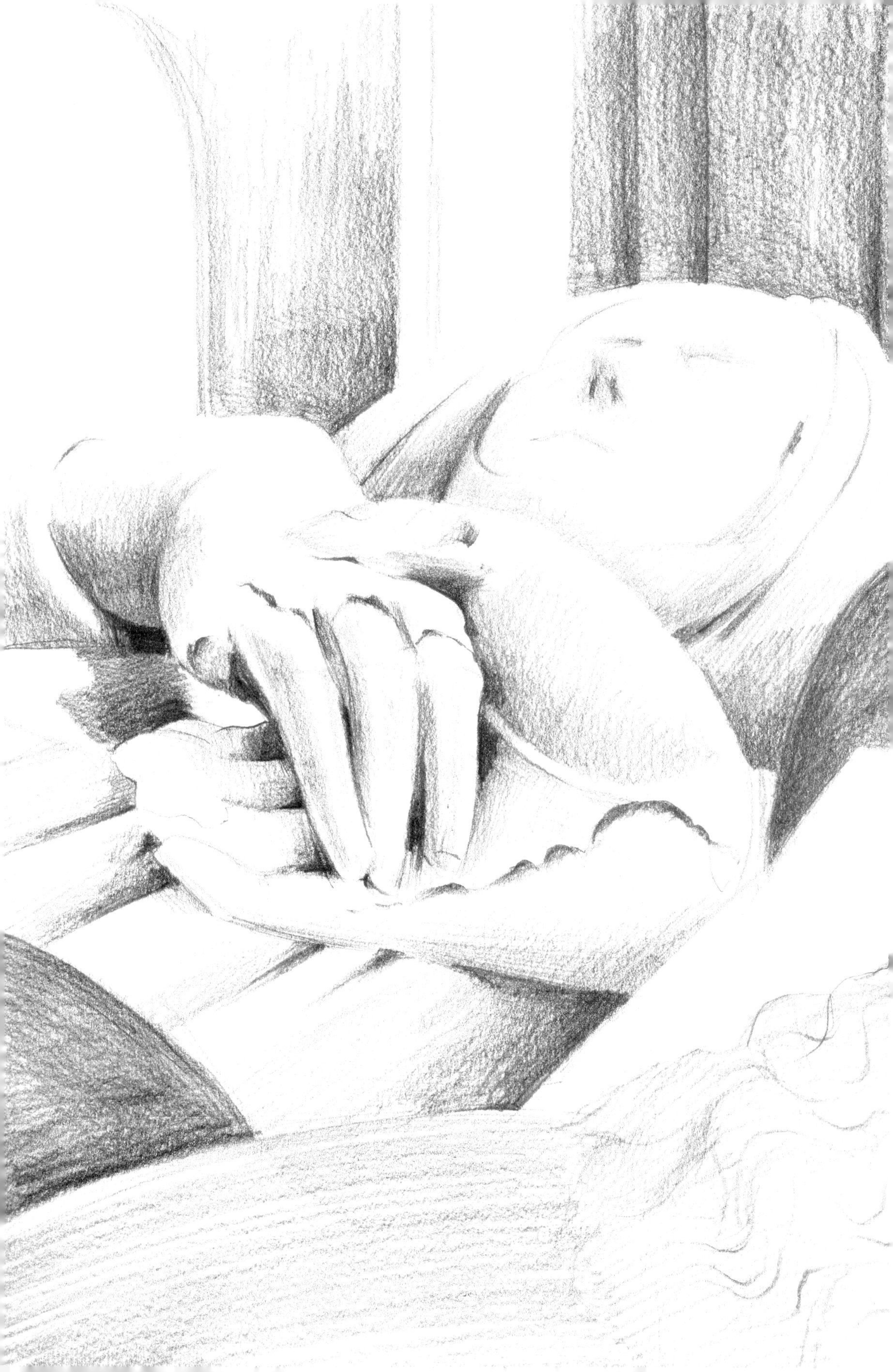

In Memoriam: Frank Smyth, Vincent Giles, Dorothy Carey, Dorothy James, November 1990

Dorothy, Dorothy, Frank, and Vincent,
Died in the fall as the leaves fell,
Vince, Damaris, Jo and Audrey,
Left behind with a tale to tell.

Lives lived out and the hills bare
Melbury Beacon in sun and shade
Air crisp and the heart sore
Hole in the ground by the autumn spade.

Sorrow stalks the down and the coombe
Over the chalk and down to the clay
Cold the wind and deep their wound
Blank the night and bleak the day.

East Melbury and Whitepit lane,
Bear the wheels of the silent car
Pools by the roadside shine with rain
Mud lies streaky on gravel and tar.

Melbury's dead are waiting for friends
Exalted in grief by the ancient words
At the filled front pew the long years end
In the organ's clatter of chords.

When the silent valleys were waters and wide
And round them the great hills smoothed and sank
Ancient folk roamed them, suffered and died
Like Dorothy, Dorothy, Vincent and Frank.

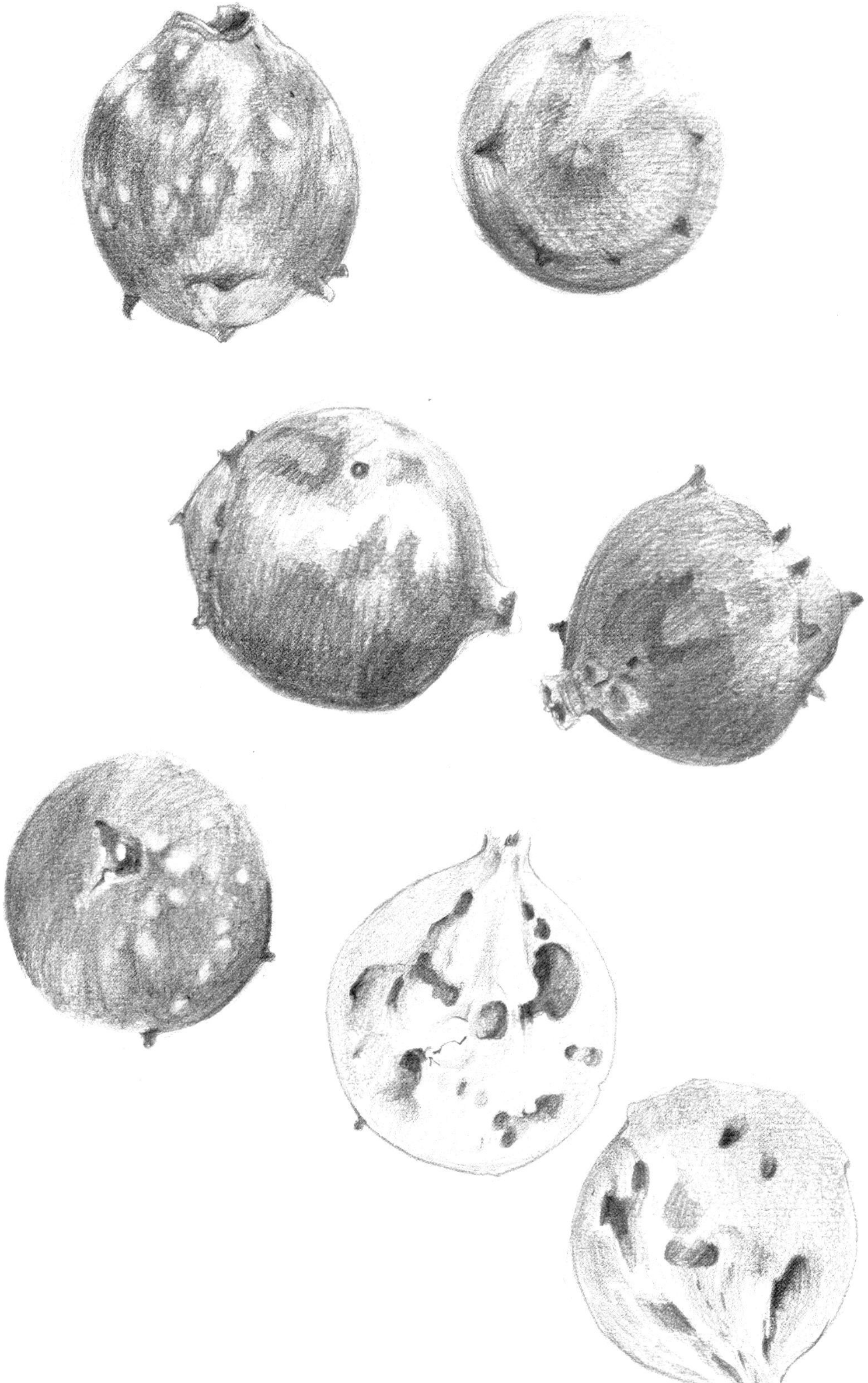

Late November

Weeping indeed the willow and the pear
Shedding raindrops for lost summers
Into a garden once rich with bloom
Stricken by man and early frost.
Cut to the earth are the bushes
So lately red with berries
Now black with compost
The helianthemums lie near death
So distant is the sun.

Misty and messy lies the long lawn
Fallen leaves curled into cups holding rain
Birch twigs without order, logic, shape
Lie on the grass muddy as the lane.

But the wild west winds -
Surely the poet said,
They hint at spring not far behind?
Wrong! Just wild west wind driven across cold heights.
The light browns
Threatening rain through long dark nights.

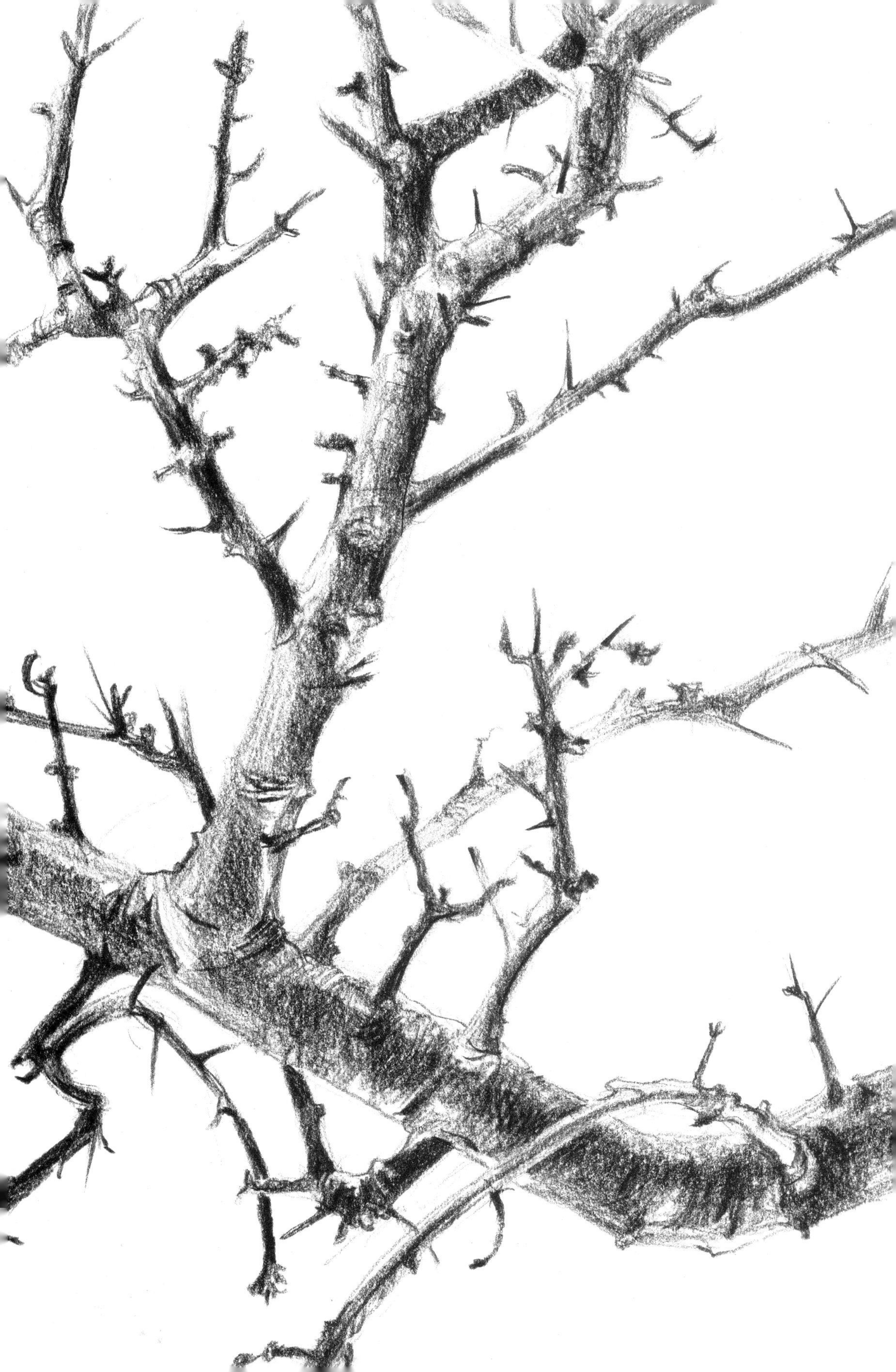

Black Dog

The small birds have gone,
With the leaves of an empty garden
In an early descent of night.
Nothing happens though the earth revolves
Its crew clutching the surface
They pass each other in a long street
Silent in the bustle of business
Secrets of the despair are locked in hearts
That cannot remember how to speak of them.

Ask the doctor what can fill such empty spaces
How to enter again the sunlit lawn
Where friendly children run between the stumps
And the red roses nod in rhythm.
Alien shores? They roar in equal desolation
Music, even, repeats its tired themes
Will the finches and the leaf ever return
Or the distant sea grow blue in rhapsody?

Only the secret movements of the heart
Will shake this brown dump
No deed or thought a man may have.
Wars without victories, deepen defeat.
The dog blackens.

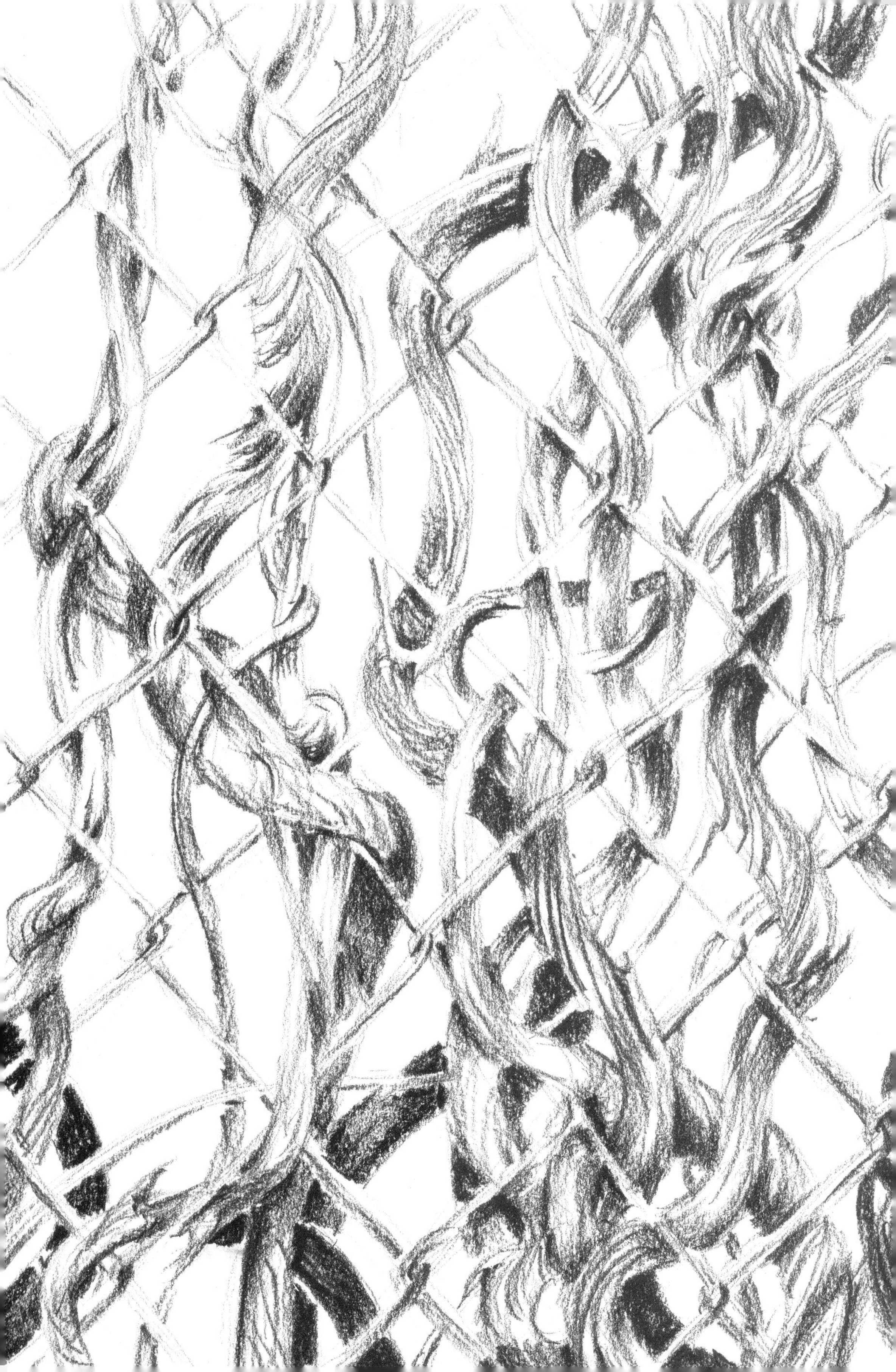

In Praise of Tennis

Tennis excludes the world and all its cares,
Money, ambition, hoping and despairs
Plays out its rituals in due proportions
Fixed, immutable, without distortions.

Beyond the confines of this neutral court
Its net so tautly drawn, and lines so finely wrought
Our lives depend on accident and chance
Too random for this measured tennis dance.

Inexorable the rules and harsh the scores
Here there's no privilege to open doors
Only the placing of the speeding ball
Brings failure and success, ascent or fall.

Though luck rides in she leaves no lasting scar
All evens out and we return to par
A gentle courtesy means none complain
Alike we share the sunshine and the rain

Though mighty empires fail and skies may fall
The players hear the voice of justice call.
Rejoice then strikers of the yellow ball
In this safe world, losers, as well, take all.

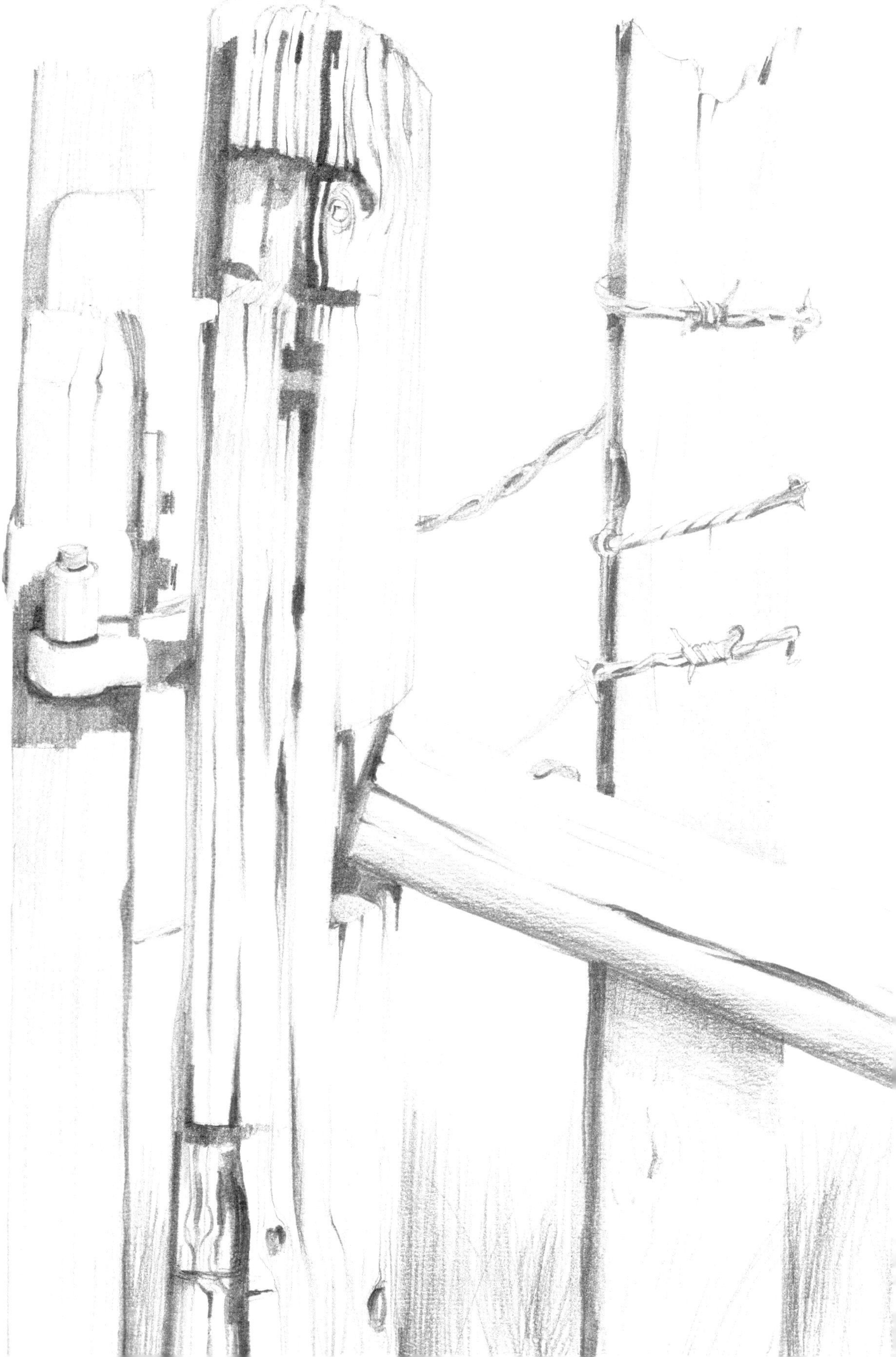

Encounter

Ugly, small, she seemed a manikin
Outward splayed her purple legs
Nose thrusting through the skin
Time had left her with life's dregs.

She saw me looking, a smile
Melted that hard face
A girl, speedy, straight and lithe
Took, just then, the old crone's place.

Clutching her bag of supermarket goodies
Her light in these dark days.
I turned into the burden of her age.
She could not stand a stranger's gaze.

We did not speak
Clutching, smiling, changing, swallowed up her day
Like the car park, vast and bleak.
We, alas, had nothing to say.

We may meet again, Shaftesbury so small
But of this day shall have no memory
Only these lines wrap up a faint recall
The grey air enfolds us separately.

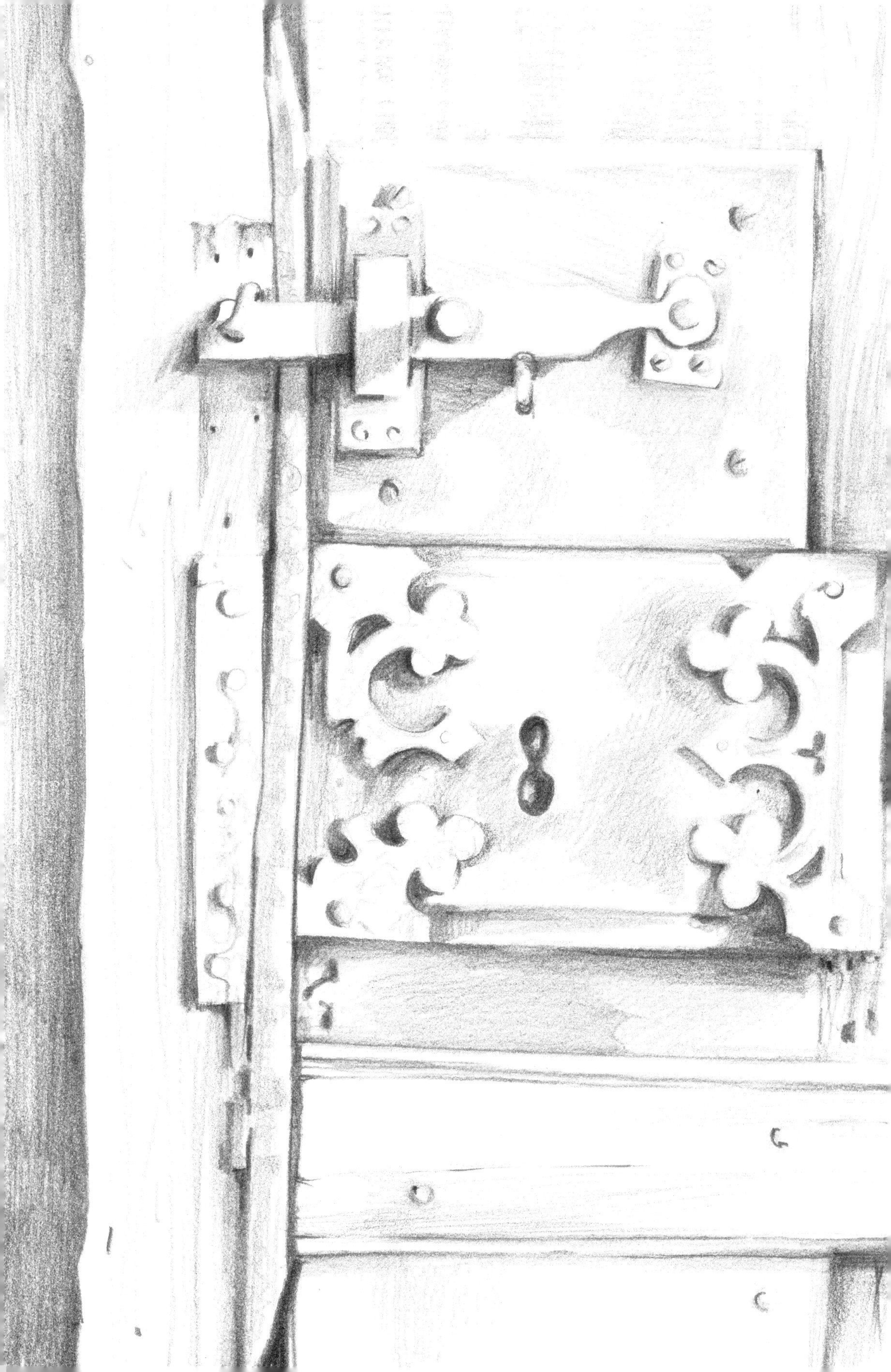

A Bird in the Road

A fearful thrush shivers on the white line,
Fallen there helpless, not its volition
Feather-roughed, blinking, threatened by tyres
Luck alone defies the final demolition.

Framed in a banging universe of cars
There in the middle, safe on that thin line?
How will it know what makes a driver swerve?
That luck holds life but only cats have nine.

We too, caught up in our situations
Run in fast lines of ruled monotony
We do not find the strength to fly away
Fearful we see no opportunity.

And yet returning, there's no shivered thrush
Of death, of feathers, blood, no single trace
Did my bird find enough of strength to fly
How else to disappear in this mad race?

WINTER

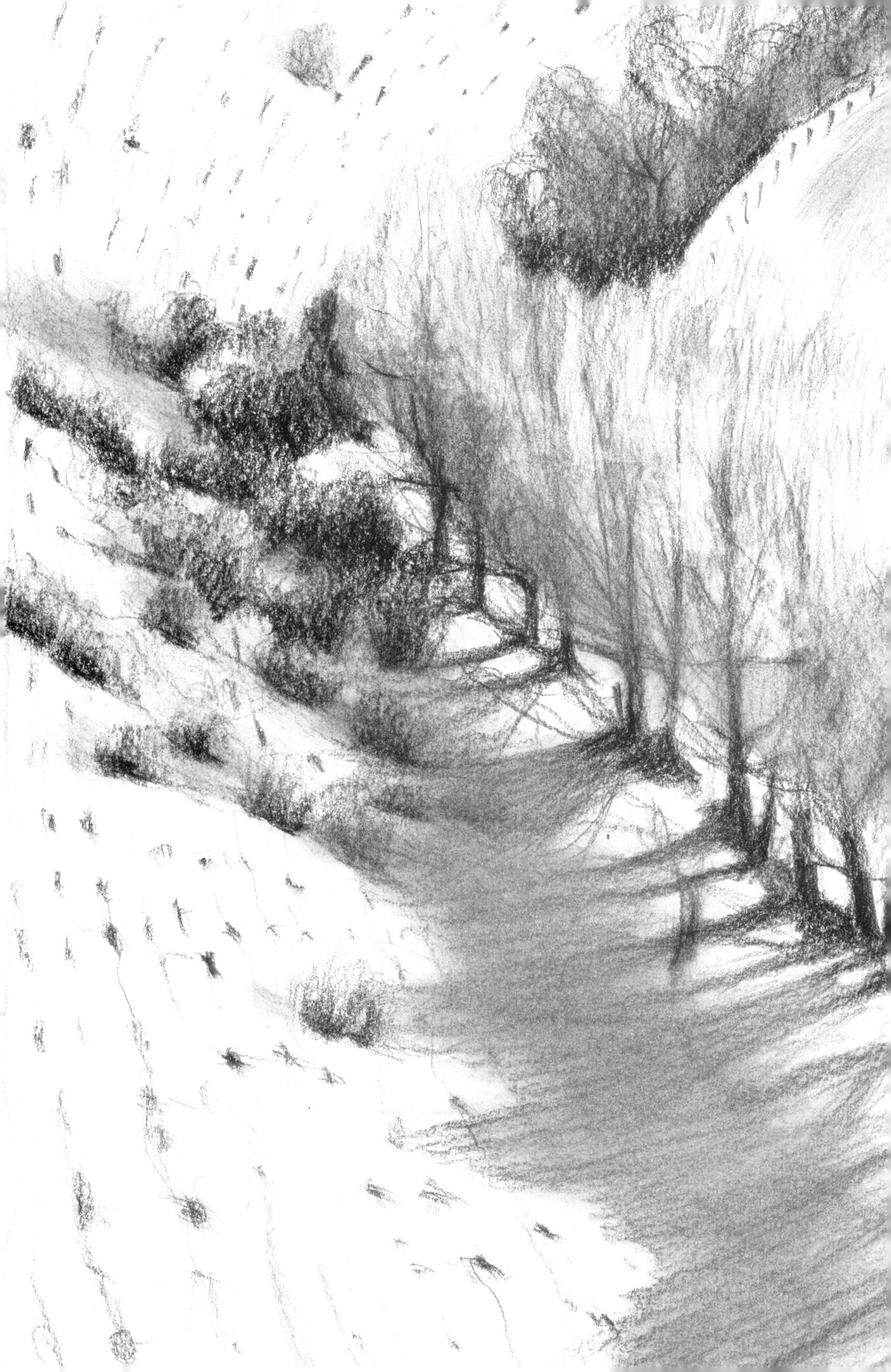

Colours in a Melbury Landscape

Morning: the sky grey
And black with swift circulations of rooks
Fields untouched by spring: matt green
Air you can hold: browns

Afternoon: the sky blue
One sun drives off a hundred rooks
Earth-born winds saunter through the old grass
Air not visible: pure vision

Evening: a moment of orange
Sunshafts folded into cloud.
Sudden, before twilight, all the colours return
Grey, green, gold, brown, black

Loveliest of all the end of day
Till darkness puts the Joseph's coat away.

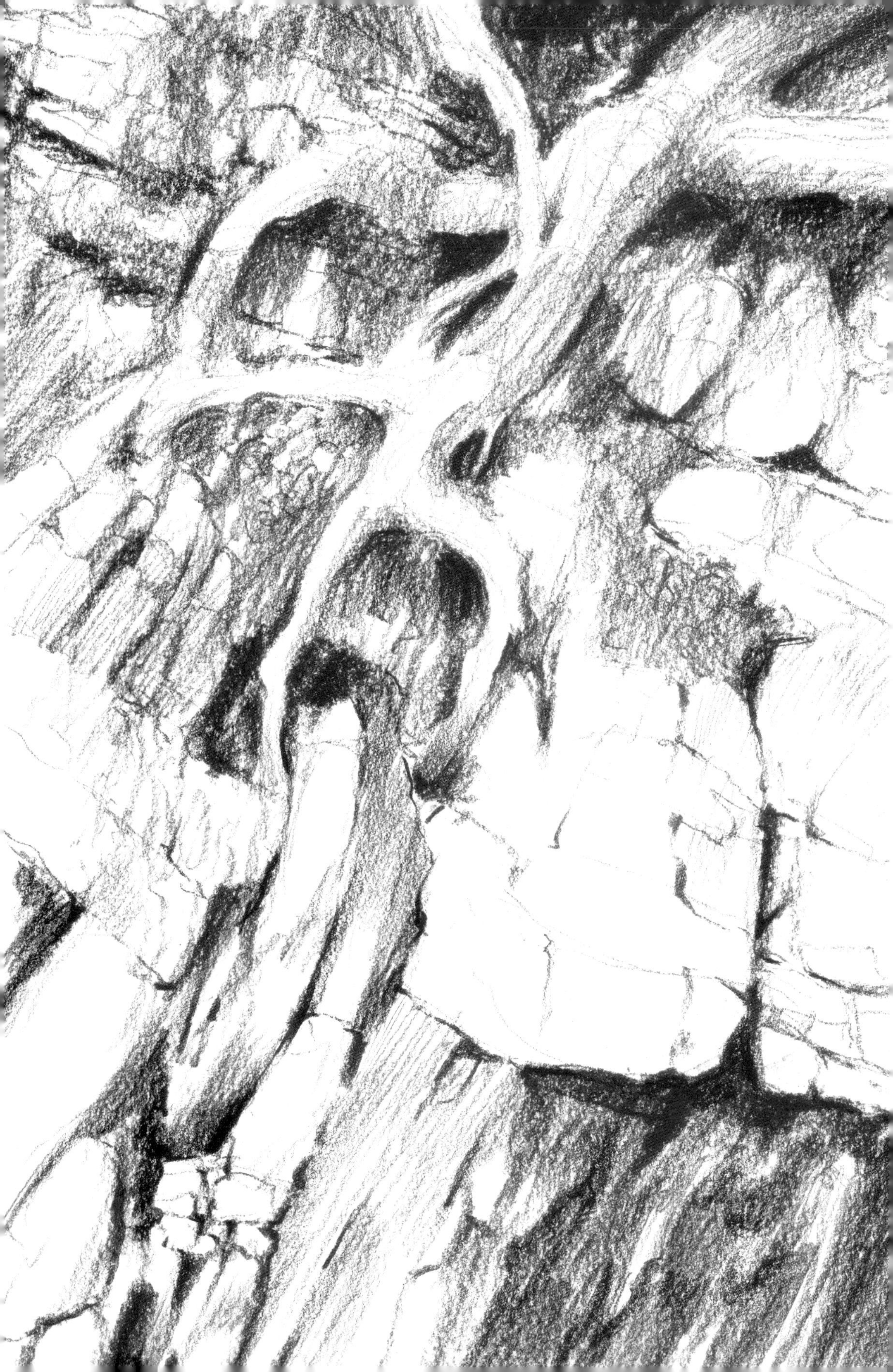

After the Great Storm

The great storm blew all night and closed the C13.
I crossed the stile, door to the secret garden
The rabbit hole to an imagined world,
Our valley turned into a different place.
No cars or tractors ran, no Cessna flew.
Silent sedges moved in leftover winds
Swayed still the barren branches, oak and ash
And small birds hid, fearful, in dark hedgerows.
I walked as in a bowl of tea, light brown,
The Jacson pond hinted at monsters down
At earth's centre. Skyward, the Beacon flared
In jockey colours, bands of black and gold.
Music here where chalky springs sang water songs
And wellingtons sucked mud from black leaf mulch.

Suddenly, silence held back the natural night
As other worlds gleamed from valley slopes
Drawing from greensand beds and long dead bones
The murmurings of the ancient sounds
Mouthed by peoples heard here long ago.
And others from the stones beside the church
Which westward looks across the Blackmore Vale.

As the red clearance vehicles arrive
And traffic threads again its race and roar
The valley voices silent fall, this land
Comes back to us and all is as before.

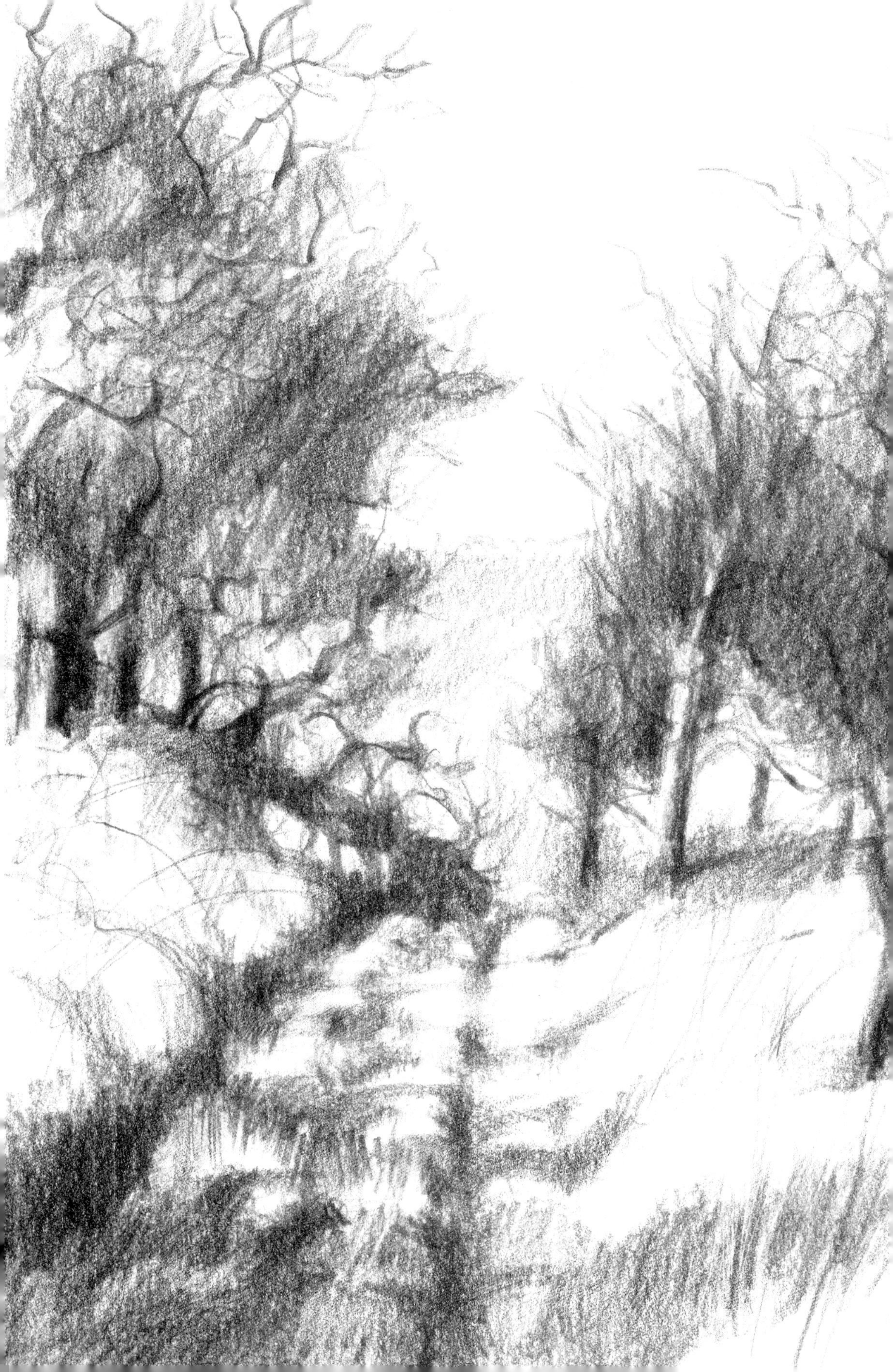

December Day

Brown air clamped the landscape
Held it immobile though winds blew low
From that bare prison, no escape
Offered that a man might know.

It seemed a cosmic shoot had taken place
No cattle, dogs, sheep even
Mysteriously vanished in this waste
No leaf, crow nor sparrow tumbled about heaven.

There was no menace; no chasms gape
No waves roared in through helpless fields
No snow, thunder, volcanic rape
No grinding glacier where all nature yields

No, just that deadness which so flatly lies
When the sun, the light has gone away
All ends, the world dies
Endless, desolate, inexplicable is this day.

Rugby on TV: Ireland v. England

President and personages parade
They too observe the rhythm of the bands
Players like soldiers for battle all arrayed
Gladiators, affront the roaring stands.

Silence falls as all are introduced
A little joke, a politician's smile
They bend or nod and tightened lips are loosed
As great ones move along the file.
Spectators sway with patriotic hope
They stretch to the horizon like the dead
Viewing the pitch as through a telescope
Across a pit of seventy thousand heads.

For a second a sacred silence holds
President, players , crowds and viewers in communion
A tranquil beauty every heart enfolds
Space, Time, Occasion, all in union.
We wait within this universe to hear
The voice of God proclaim salvation
Heads bowed in reverence and fear
This Judgement day of Revelation.

The whistle breaks illusion
The players shatter truce
Taking position in precise confusion.
Friendly partisans resume abuse.

The game? Well, the usual thrusting haunches
A little ball, muddied on the floor
'A terrible beauty is born' the scrum half launches
The green river to a score.

After the victory, the humbled and the proud
After the cheering and beyond the tears
A field with posts lies empty of its crowd.
Each man fights again his customary fears.

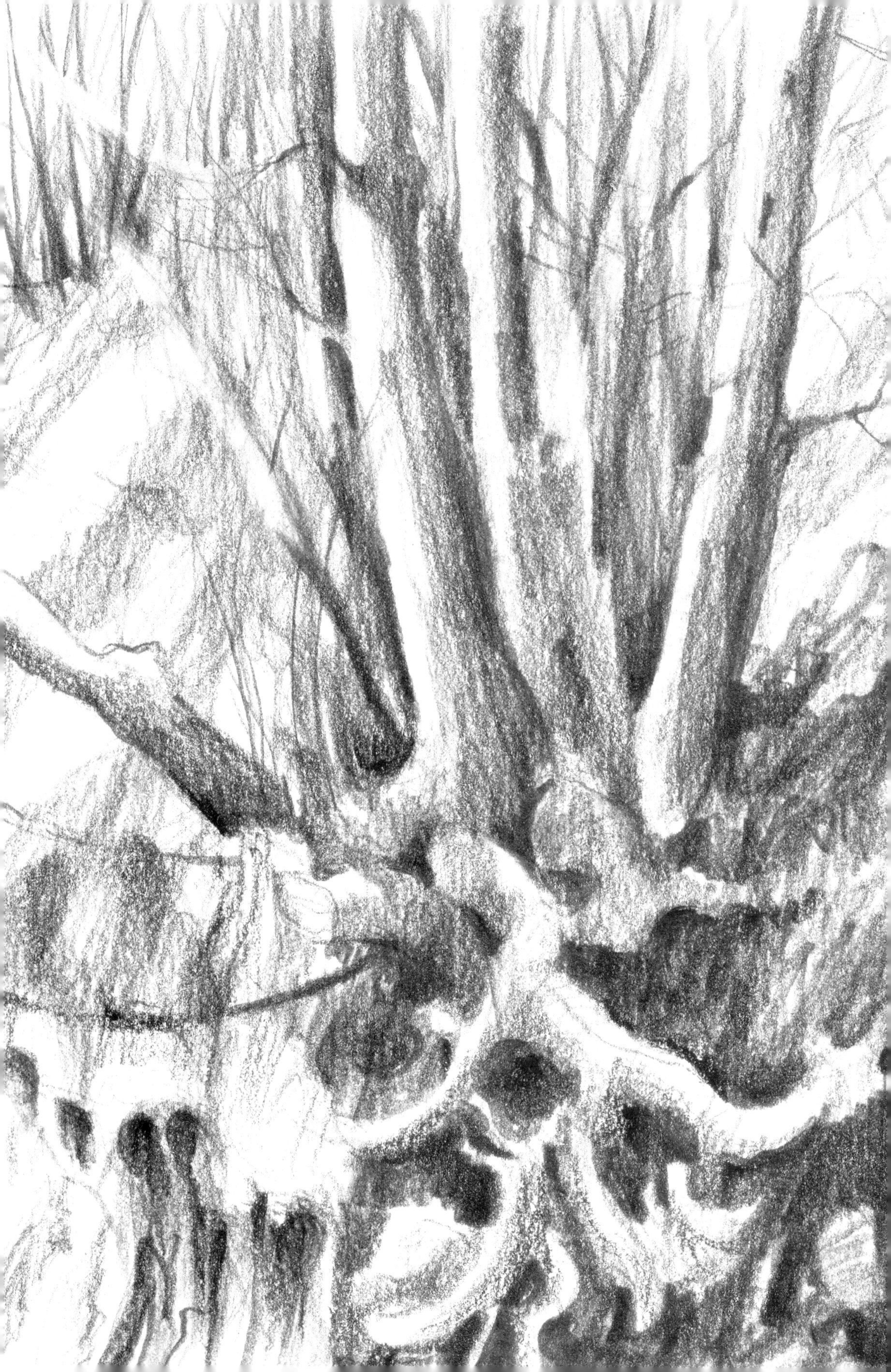

The Day They Took the Calves Away

Cows grieve like the tuning of a big brass band
One note held by tuba, trumpet, horn
The bandsmen, black, white and brown
Packed close, yet solitary and forlorn.

Two hours of lamentation brings hunger back anew
They must accept a loss that nothing can restore
Scattering they resume their dedicated chew
Everything for them is as before.

Around the browsing beasts
New instruments take up the music's line
Crows inject discordant bass
And distant campanologists a tenor rime

To gentle winds my earpiece yields
Make whispers bang like wild seas
Mud sucks at boots in soggy fields
Staccato punctuation of melodic trees.

The cows ignore the jolting symphony
Allegro, andante, presto all the same
Withdraw their brass, percussion, timpani
Crunching, munching, their world reclaim.

These sounds rumbling through the Melbury bowl
Eight thousand years of joys and ills
Since grinding ice and wolf pack howl
God, man and beast resound from Dorset hills.

Silences

It was your going, not out on rough seas
Nor sitting by the waters of Babylon
Nor taking off, out of our human air

Just across the tiling to the garage.

You would not stay long, just for five minutes
To find that quiche lurking in the freezer
I stayed inside, happy to be useful
Winkling out pips from seville oranges
For mighty making of the marmalade.

It was the silence.
Not the silence of ceased conversation,
Or which follows a light sleep after lunch
The juggling with the jig-saw pieces
Or when we put the red photinia in.
These are absences, spaces without noise.
As if the spheres themselves had gone to sleep.
But all stays totally familiar
Your remaining entirely as before.

When you go out that is a happening
The world changes, it becomes another
Yet old as if we had begun again
Losing the glories of our fifty years
If you died that is how the world would be.

Other silences we hear and touch
Solid, substantial, positive, events and things:
The sheep, cylindrical barrels on thin sticks
A Shetland pony tied to alien soil
Under trees, all standing so still, windless in winter.
The pause between Allegro and Andante,
Before doomed Hamlet drinks the poisoned cup
Or at the breaking of long-stayed friendships.

When you return, waving the obscure quiche
Pleased to find fruit ready for the cutting
Such ordinary things dispel the pain
Silence may safely cover us again.

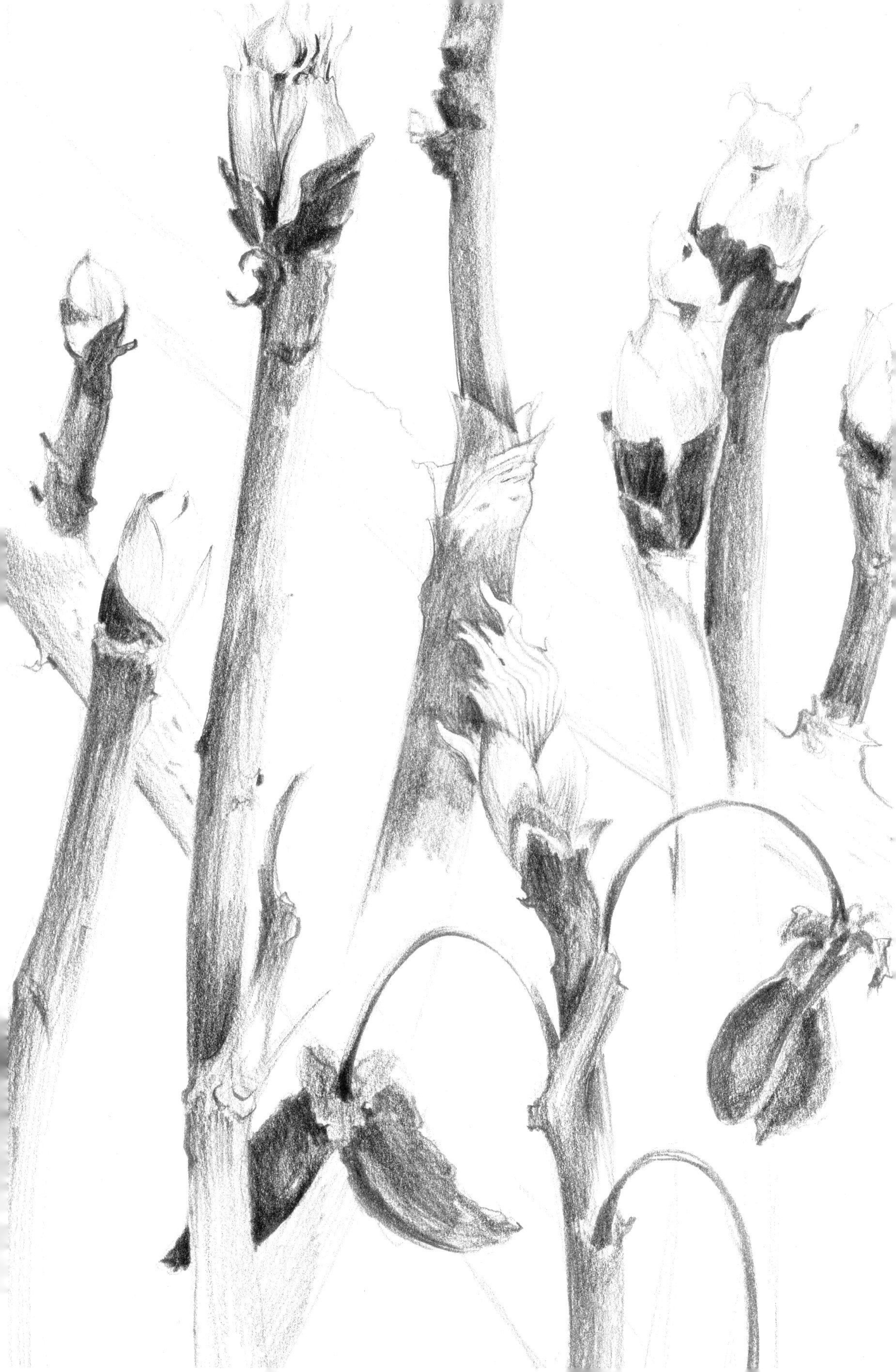

Spring Delays

Spring must wait upon the weather vane
Here in our Melbury this February day
Clouds build defences for a lengthy stay
North east a wind jackboots down Charlton Lane.
Parades of pigeons dip across the plain
Arrows launched at Agincourt's fierce fray.
But little birds, mistaking seasons, stray
From friendly hedges, to their soft refrain.

Ambiguous such signs, they have no strength
Spring's early intimations quickly blighted
Even as the drab grass moves, the winter's length
Asserts itself in windows early lighted.
Yet cows in sheds cry out for airy fields
And dream of frolics when the winter yields

Four Sunsets…

October
In a black western sky
A long light streak opens and the sun's glow
Goldens all from Beacon to Breeze hill
Topping the Caterpillar beech in its rich flow

November
The year's best, this one, a great prize
All happening at once and staying longer
Thirty minutes before all dies.
Low in the east, a gibbous moon, God's fist
Hangs over Zig-Zag in a samite mist
West lies the sun on Melbury hill
Turning it orange then red
Rests for a moment on a turquoise bed.
Man intrudes, a plane beyond our sight
Leaves a ruled line fading into height.
Who arranged this symmetry
Both globes poised in one blue sky?

December
An orange sun, dappled by clouds
Hangs, a balloon, over Compton Down
By Zig-Zag, where I stand, winter closes
Looming suddenly from Eastern hills

Another December
The sky is a Red Sea
Parted, by a black strip, waves
Glowing, another miracle.
Further, bloodier red, a mountain
Threatens explosion, until .
The cosmic bulb which lit the show sinks
Lingers a moment on the Beacon, then
Dark swallows all.

…and a Sunrise

The Year's Last Day
Dun cloud drifts east and high
Sun levels out behind Breeze hill
Sends rays to make an orange sky
God glowing softly in the air he fills.

Our fourteen trunks of coppiced ash
Lacily decorate the clouds' long flow
Forty rooks a black-blood sash
Break, dive, claw up, go.

Now over Compton Down the greyer cloud
Edged only with the east's spare rays
A dead man's shroud
Folded around this last of days.

And west, where skies and Melbury Beacon meet
The orange east just tips the scrubby top
North, the cloud-made Himalayan peaks
Seal off our universe and this year stops.

Envoi

We love them so, sunset and sunrise
Knowing how the stories end
But do not end
Soon there will be tomorrow
Tomorrow will be tomorrow's year
Deep in our hearts we know
That we have nothing to fear.

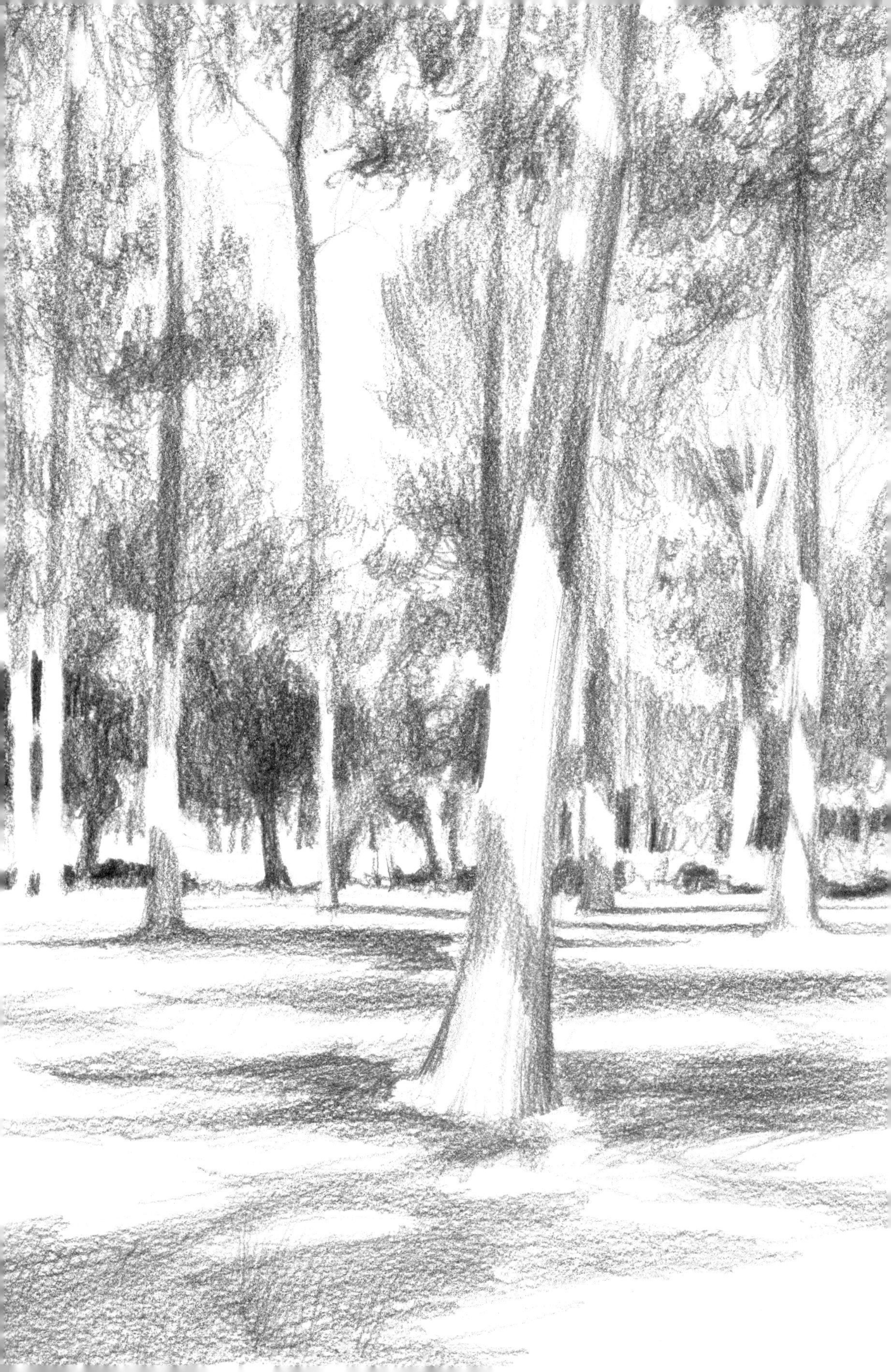

Sue, on her Eightieth Birthday

You are a tree, all the trees
In our garden where the birds sing
A silver birch, running free
With the breezes of the spring.

And the tough, the upright sort
Turning aside the autumn gale
Untroubled stands the stalwart oak
Steady the broad-leaf lime though branches flail

Like too the pretty ones, acer drummondii
Green with golden foliage blend
Ash too, its branches brush the sky
Snake-bark maple, small birds' friend.

You are an evergreen at eighty
Shield our nest from winter's claw
With your beeches at the gateway
Young as the winter jasmine by the wall.

Through summer branches children squeeze
We shade ourselves, pretend to read
You are all these lovely trees
Their pleasure and their joyful need.

Though leaves must fall
The trees live long
And so to you I offer all
These poems say, our true love song.

DRAWINGS

Page　　　　*Title*

Endpapers	Ancient lime tree
2	Logs: leaves
4	St. Thomas, Melbury Abbas
6	Frosted magnolias. 2008
8	Neolithic ditch, Breeze Hill
10	Garden gate; 'caterpillar' plantation
12	Scrap
14	Double portrait: National Museum of Wales
16	Angel; St. Thomas, Melbury Abbas
18	Nun, St. Thomas, Melbury Abbas
20	Birches in Bob and Sue's garden
24	Sunlight, Melbury Wood
28	Apple tree, lawn; Stour Provost
30	'Bacchante' sculpture of A. Pajou. 1774
32	Fresh fish, from Joseph Stannard. 1825
34	Water iris
36	Sarah's border, Edwardstowe
38	The Track, Breeze Hill
40	Victorian lady's linen gloves

42	Fishermen's knots, Bardsey Island
44	Pines in Juliet's garden
48	Picnic, King's Park, Perth W.A.
50	Rooks
52	Badger sett, Castle Hill, Shaftesbury
54	Zig-Zag Hill
56	The Aundel tomb, Chichester Cathedral
58	Wasp galls, Jimena
60	Thorn twig
62	Honeysuckle, Parry's court
64	Field posts, Lundy Island
66	Locks, St. Illtyd's Chapel, Caldey
70	Breeze Hill, the west valley
72	Roots; chalk
74	The track to Melbury Wood
78	Sycamore roots, Breeze Hill
82	Buds of Paeonia Lutea
86	White poplars in sunlight
Endpapers	Ancient lime tree

Sponsors

We are indebted to the generosity of our sponsors, supporters and donors for their essential contributions to the costs of publication.

Anon-13
P Ashby-Martin
C Austin
J & P Ballam
S & D Beaton
C & B Bowen
S & C Bracey
Breach family, Bramley
Breach family, Newbury
Breach family, Petts Wood
A Brooks
N & A Brownsell
J Cooper
J & J Coupe
J & R Crichton
T & I Crump
S Daddy
C d'Cruz
J & P Deeker
G & P Dolan
J & M Douglas
J & A Dreaper
R Edwards
H Gamper
J Griffith
B Hallaway
P Handley
B & M Harding
L Herbert
M & R Hobrough
S Howard
W E Kingswell
M Kitchen
A & N Law
P Lidsey
P & P Lloyd
A & B Lyle
J Mackay
J & C Mawer
K & M Milburn
R Montsarrat
B Morgan
K Morgan
M & N Nunan
C Pass
R & L Phillips

A Powell
F Preedy
D & E Prichard
G Purbrick
M Purcell
N Roberts
C & J Robinson
P & J Rogers
D & J Roscow
S & A Rutter
J Sargent

M Seymour
J Schofield
D Smyth
J & F Stanford
J Stoate
M C Stone
G & P Tapper
P Tate
J Whittaker
P & S White

BUSINESS SPONSORS

Shirley Allum
Country Kitchens
Hine & Parsons

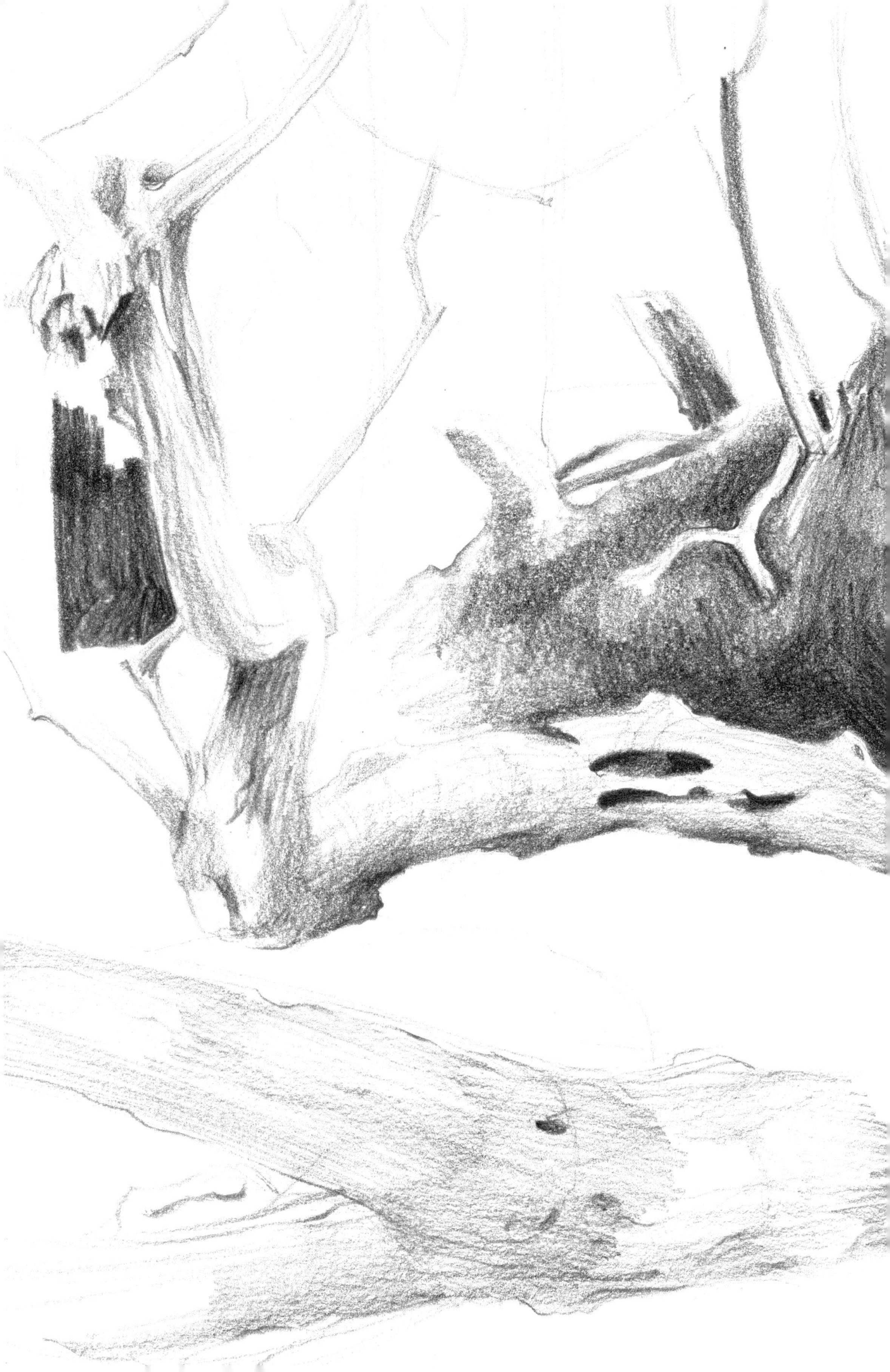

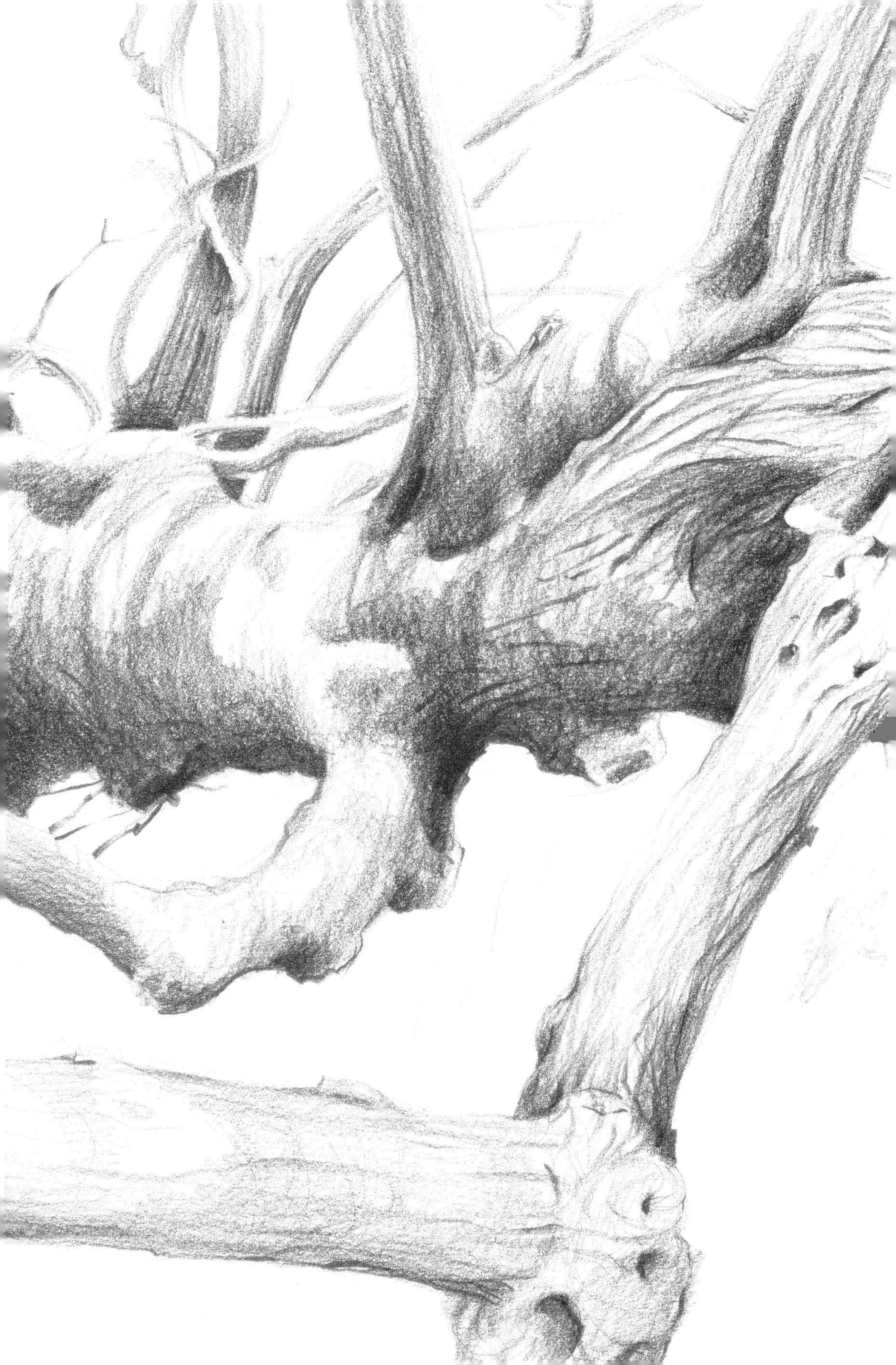